# Cops Under Fire

# COPS UNDER FIRE

## The reign of terror against hero cops

*Larry McShane*

Since 1947
**REGNERY PUBLISHING, INC.**
*An Eagle Publishing Company • Washington DC*

COPYRIGHT © 1999 Larry McShane

Library of Congress Cataloging-in-Publication Data

McShane, Larry.
   Cops under fire : the reign of terror against hero cops / Larry McShane.
     p.   cm.
   Includes index.
   ISBN 0-89526-357-2 (alk. paper)
   1. Police community relations—United States—Case studies.
   2. Police shootings—United States—Case studies. 3. Police
discretion—United States—Case studies. 4. Police and the press-
-United States—Case studies. 5. Police—United States—Public
opinion—Case studies. 6. Public opinion—United States—Case
studies.    I. Title.
   HV7936.P8M37   1998
   363.2'32'0973—dc21                98-48035
                                     CIP

Published in the United States by
Regnery Publishing, Inc.
One Massachusetts Avenue, NW
Washington, DC 20001

Distributed to the trade by
National Book Network
4720-A Boston Way
Lanham, MD 20706

Printed on acid-free paper.
Manufactured in the United States of America

10 9 8 7 6 5 4 3 2 1

Books are available in quantity for promotional or premium use. Write to Director of Special Sales, Regnery Publishing, Inc., One Massachusetts Avenue, NW, Washington, DC 20001, for information on discounts and terms or call (202) 216-0600.

For my wife Marjorie and our three children
Stacey, Megan, and Joseph.

# CONTENTS

## Acknowledgments

Thanks to Al Regnery and everyone at Eagle Publishing for their help and confidence in a first-time author; thanks to Ed Hayes, who made it all possible; thanks to Rick Hampson, Jerry Schwartz, Richard Pyle, and Bob Hardt, good friends who always offered better advice; thanks to all the guys in parking lot 17-D, Giants Stadium; and most of all, thanks to the officers whose stories are told in this book, and to the lawyers who defended them, for their patience and cooperation. Thanks to my parents, Jack and Nora McShane, for a lifetime of love and support.

*Chapter One*

# SECOND-GUESSING

**IT'S ALWAYS ABOUT** second-guessing. You're riding in a patrol car through a particularly nasty stretch of urban America—Bed-Stuy in Brooklyn, Watts in Los Angeles, downtown Detroit—near the end of a drowsy midnight-to-eight tour. Or maybe you're in some suburb, a low-crime oasis—Cedar Grove, New Jersey, or Revere, Massachusetts—places where cops can go a whole career without ever unholstering their weapon, and you're questioning a burglary suspect on an otherwise quiet afternoon.

And something happens. It could be a big something—the pop-pop-pop of a 9mm emptying somewhere nearby, or a suspect making a move toward your weapon. It could be a small something—a routine radio call, a traffic stop, or a suspicious-looking lowlife (a "skell" in police parlance) standing in the wrong place at the wrong time. It could be happening somewhere else—as you're driving quietly along, somebody one town over steals a car and makes a wrong turn and winds up on your turf.

It doesn't happen to a lot of cops. In New York City, for example, there are 38,000 police officers assigned to protect a population of more than 7,000,000 people. Only 250 have ever used their weapons in the line of duty three times—less than one-tenth of 1 percent. The odds that it won't happen at all are very, very good.

But when it does happen, it will change your life forever.

It doesn't matter how it happens. If it does happen, it will be over in a matter of minutes, maybe even a matter of seconds. Its repercussions will echo for years and years.

A woman named Strawberry happened to Officer Robert Leaks of the Newark Police Department one summer night in 1997. Strawberry had a long police rap sheet, and a taste for cocaine. It was the latter that drew Leaks, who moved in to make a simple street corner drug arrest. But Strawberry tried to hijack a police car, dragging Leaks along for the most frightening (and nearly the last) ride of his life. Within minutes, Strawberry was dead—killed by a single gunshot fired by Officer Leaks, who was forced to take her life to save his own. It was the first time he had ever shot his service revolver on duty.

Before a grand jury determined it was a case of justifiable homicide, Leaks's name was dragged through the mud by everybody from the victim's friends and family, to members of a notorious reputed drug gang, to the mayor of Newark. The shooting became a racial/political football, and everyone in the game lined up to kick Leaks. The way his case was handled, it became clear that politics took precedence over job performance, and so his supporters railed.

That scenario is familiar to Officers Larry Nevers and Walter Budzyn of the Detroit police. One minute they're subduing a possible drug suspect outside a crackhouse in a rugged section of the Motor City in 1992. Hours later, they watch the mayor of Detroit announce on national television that they, along with five other officers who arrested the drug suspect, are murderers.

The other five cops were never convicted of anything; most wound up collecting healthy settlements from the city after suing the mayor for his summary judgments. Nevers and Budzyn were not quite so lucky.

These two plainclothes detectives battled with suspect Malice Green on November 5, 1992. Both were con-

**Guilt or innocence is a question that can be answered by a jury. An officers' reputation? That's harder to determine or protect.**

victed, after controversial trials, of second-degree murder. Both recently had their convictions overturned, but Budzyn was subsequently convicted of involuntary manslaughter. Both continue to fight to clear their names despite spiraling legal bills. Support from their families and friends has helped them cope with the dark days and the deepening costs.

Ahh, legal bills. Restoring your reputation does not come cheaply in these days of $500-an-hour lawyers. The cost can climb well into six figures for the simplest defense case; it increases exponentially as the case goes through the lengthy appeals process. Criminal trials are only part of the problem; most of those are accompanied by civil suits filed by arrestees looking for a payday. Since many police officers are routinely underpaid, the money needed to defend yourself can be devastating to the family budget, the mortgage, the food bills.

Just ask Ramiro Pena.

Pena, a twenty-seven-year-old cop in Grand Rapids, Michigan, wound up in court trying to clear his name, too. A routine traffic stop of a car with stolen license plates turned violent when the driver sped off with two cops hanging from the wildly careening car. Pena, rushing to the aid of his fellow officers, helped arrest the driver by following official police procedure—and was rewarded with charges of aggravated assault. Before he was even charged, Pena was suspended—without pay—for seven weeks. The threat of a civil suit also hangs over Pena, another guaranteed bank account buster. Officer Leaks is facing possible civil action, as well.

Pena endured despite the fact that his bosses offered little support in the face of community protests—a pain virtually all of these officers have felt.

Pena would love to have a jury decide his case as it did that of Officer John Vojtas in one of the highest-profile cases of alleged police brutality in this decade. Jon Gammage, the cousin of Pittsburgh Steelers defensive lineman Ray Seals, died after fighting with police during a routine traffic stop in a Pittsburgh suburb.

Five cops were involved in the fatal wrestling match on the side of a highway outside Pittsburgh. The Seals connection helped make this national news, catapulting the fight between police and Gammage into a referendum on racism. Jesse Jackson was among the many black leaders who weighed in, comparing the case to the lynching of blacks in the Deep South.

But there was no evidence—nada, zero, zip—that showed John Vojtas had any racial animus against Gammage or anybody else. Vojtas was acquitted of involuntary manslaughter. Two other cops, Lt. Milton Mullholland and Officer Michael Albert, are still facing charges. After a pair of mistrials, one because of the possibly deliberate misstatement of a prosecution witness, the officers will go on trial for the third time in the death of Jon Gammage. Their lawyers are trying to block this, arguing that another trial on the same charges would amount to double jeopardy.

Alexander Lindsay, the attorney who co-defended Vojtas along with lawyer Jim Ecker, says such police cases come complete with their very own "mythology" created by instant communication. Misstatements and rumor, repeated over and over during the life of a case, create a set of "facts" about what happened that are all too often inaccurate. Stories are spread through the internet, on talk radio, on television, in the media. Few people bother to check these assertions, content to accept as fact what they read or hear about the case.

"A lot of the story just becomes an ongoing myth," says Lindsay. "If you read the editorials about the Gammage case, it always comes back to this: Five police officers got on top of him and held him down. Well, that just didn't happen." And he adds that those perceptions can be countered by the truth once you seat a jury.

Convincing twelve people is easier than convincing the general public, as Blake Hubbard found out. Hubbard had his day in court and walked out a free man—but nothing was

really the same. He became Dallas (Texas) County's first officer tried on job-related murder charges in more than two
decades. His "crime"? Hubbard shot an emotionally disturbed man who ignored repeated requests to drop a knife
before lunging with the weapon at another officer.

Such a decision exacts a psychological toll on the officer,
one that is often ignored in the myriad investigations that follow any police shooting. "I'm living with it every day," he says
now. "And I will every day of my life."

Although Hubbard was initially backed by his superiors,
their support evaporated when the local chapter of the
NAACP began protesting the shooting. He is now familiar
with that feeling of isolation that becomes natural to a cop on
trial. Hubbard, the fourth generation in his family to enter
law enforcement, is fighting in court to get his job back—not,
he says, that he really has any choice in the matter.

"It's an extremely horribly expensive deal for my family,"
says Hubbard. "But how can you say I can't afford to defend
myself? How can you say I should go to prison?"

You see, there's always somebody second-guessing.

Everybody has an opinion, from the elected officials, to
the newspaper columnists, to the voices on the radio, to the
guy on the street corner. Everybody has a question—not that
they all have an interest in hearing your answer.

Why did he stop that car? Why did he have to pull the
trigger? Was the shooting justified? Why did this have to happen in an election year? How can we make the protestors go
away? What's the best way to "spin" this thing? Was this a
racial incident—black and white?

They ignore all the grays.

David H. Martin, an ex-Justice Department official and the head of the Law Enforcement Legal Defense Fund, puts it this way: "This anxiety of being second-guessed by superiors, prosecutors, and judges is a sad reality that police officers face daily." The result? "There is a tendency not to take risks in difficult arrest situations which were once considered routine," Martin says.

The cop looks for support, but he finds second-guessers. Even in his own department, the incident will be investigated thoroughly, his every decision—made under extreme duress in the blink of an eye—will be questioned from the comfortable perspective of hindsight. Public opinion will play a role; politics will play an even bigger one.

**The suspension was typical of the way police officers rarely receive the constitutional rights routinely accorded the people they arrest: the presumption of innocence, the right to a fair trial.**

Rank-and-file cops from coast to coast say the fallout from these police brutality cases is a less effective police force. It's a tough job under ordinary circumstances; it's become extraordinarily difficult under a microscope.

Fred LeMaire is a union official in Michigan, where Pena, Nevers, and Budzyn all went on trial. The cases have had a chilling effect on officers in that state, he says.

"It gives you a tendency to say, 'Why get involved? If I do, I'm always facing second-guessing, armchair quarterbacking,'" LeMaire says, "whether that's the correct attitude or not."

Check out these figures from Los Angeles in the wake of the Rodney King case. Use of force arrests were down 31 percent in the three years after the highly-publicized case from 1990. Uses of police-issued batons were down 90 percent from 1990 to 1994, an indication that cops didn't want to wind up in the same docket as Sgt. Stacey Koon and his three codefendants.

LeMaire is not alone in his position.

"American justice has turned into a system where politics and race can frustrate fairness and truth," former U.S. Attorney General Edwin Meese observed after watching the two Rodney King trials. Jack McEntee, a police union official in Newark, New Jersey, puts it more directly.

"The people who put the most amount of scrutiny on police officers, on the best day of their lives, couldn't do what we routinely do on a daily basis," McEntee says. "They sit there, all these lawyers and judges, and they Monday morning quarterback while they're sitting in a well-lit living room.

"We don't have that luxury."

Not at all. Jack Healy, vice president of the New York City Police Detectives Endowment Association, said many of his members go to work every day knowing they might never return home.

"Unfortunately, it's the nature of the beast," he said in January 1998, when an NYPD detective was killed during a buy-and-bust operation that went sour. "The dealers know the cops wear a vest. All they have to do is pat him on the back, and he's got a big problem."

It used to be that a police officer received the benefit of the doubt. Not any more.

Who was on trial in Los Angeles after the murders of Ron Goldman and Nicole Brown—O. J. Simpson or the Los Angeles Police Department? The defense turned the trial upside down, and Simpson walked out a free man from a trial that had once seemed sure to end with his conviction on two counts of murder.

Dante, in his tale about the levels of Hell, had nothing on an accused cop. They endure their own private Hades, with its own painful levels: The Incident. The Allegations. The Investigation. The Grand Jury. The Indictment. And sometimes, The Trial. And always, The Aftermath— the part where Humpty Dumpty can never be put back together again.

**Before any charges were filed, before any investigation was completed, the Rev. Jesse Jackson was comparing the death to an old-fashioned "lynching," as if the KKK had stopped him and thrown a rope over a tree alongside Route 51.**

One decision can affect literally thousands of lives. If Rodney King had pulled over and surrendered to the police, would Los Angeles have burned? Would two veteran cops have gone to jail?

Sometimes the answers give no relief. A traffic cop on Long Island pulls over a driver who was speeding and weaving down the Long Island Expressway. The driver gets out and pulls a gun. When he refuses to drop the weapon and advances toward the officer, the cop is forced to shoot.

The gun turned out to be fake. The driver was a suicidal teen with a $6,000 gambling debt. He left behind a note explaining how he wanted to be killed by a police officer.

"Suicide by cop" is how the psychologists described it. That doesn't make it any easier for the shooter to handle.

A cop doesn't need a national audience and a videotaped incident to wind up on trial. Detective Zaher Zahrey of the New York Police Department was done in by a single phone call from an informant with 80-proof breath.

Zahrey had nearly a decade on the job, was a decorated police detective, and was hailed by his superiors for his leadership and skill. But in New York City in 1993, police corruption became a cause célèbre. The city was cracking down on rogue cops, and spending more money to do it. The tip from the drunk linked Zahrey to a dangerous drug gang, and threw the unwitting detective into a Kafka-esque whirl that only ended four years later with his acquittal on drug and other charges.

You see, timing matters, too. Tensions were high after the Rodney King beating when Nevers and Budzyn made their 1992 arrest in Detroit. The officers were white, the suspect was black. Due process was out, public relations was in. Nevers and Budzyn were sacrificed on the altar of public opinion, with the suspect presented—not entirely accurately, it turned out—as the helpless victim of brutal white cops, a King redux.

But no evidence of racial animus was ever introduced at trial. No proof was offered that the two cops singled out this drug suspect simply because of the color of his skin.

Again, shades of gray.

Not every cop who's put on trial is guilty; tales of brutality like the alleged beating and sexual assault of a Haitian immigrant in a Brooklyn police precinct cry out for a full investigation of the accused officers. And certainly, some police officers are guilty of crimes they will never be charged with committing. But lately, cases involving cops are often more political, more scrutinized, and more explosive than those that don't.

The officers in this book—Pena and Zahrey, Leaks and Hubbard—all wound up wearing handcuffs and sitting at the defense table, instead of testifying for the prosecution. Each case has its own twists and turns; in some cases the legal battle drags on and on, unresolved.

The cases had other similarities, other common ground.

**Scapegoating.** Hubbard and Pena absolutely believe they became easy targets for city officials in Grand Prairie, Texas, and Muskegon, Michigan, to soothe angry local activists. NYPD Detective Zahrey shares their feelings; he believes his prosecution was the result of overzealous investigators determined to justify their existence. In the higher profile cases involving Nevers/Budzyn and Mulholland and company, public outcry virtually ensured indictments; ditto the Leaks case.

**Race.** White cops, black victims—regardless of the evidence or the reality, this remains a volatile combination. No evidence of racial animus was introduced against Hubbard, yet the local NAACP became involved against him. "If I'd shot a white guy or if I was a black cop, I don't think this would be happening," Hubbard says. Ditto Nevers and Budzyn. There's also been a strange twist in racial politics— black versus blue has moved in as a replacement for black

versus white. Leaks, a black cop, shot and killed a black suspect—yet authorities discussed a possible civil rights charge
against him. Pena, a Mexican-American, was vilified by
minority groups because the suspect he forcibly arrested was
black. McEntee says there are certain groups—in the Leaks
case, a well-organized group of alleged drug dealers—bent
on undercutting the police: "I'm sure if in fact he had been
white rather than black, they would have used that, just like
they used everything else." But as police forces become more
integrated, it seems that the race of the victim is more important than the race of the officer involved. The cops are always
blue, regardless of their own personal heritage.

**Uncooperative suspects.** The LAPD's Sgt. Stacey C.
Koon, in his book *Presumed Guilty*, remembered Rodney
King as about the most frightening suspect he had encountered in his fifteen years on the force—hardly a helpless victim, as King's backers and most public opinion believed. "I
was in charge of the officers," Koon wrote. "I was not in
charge of the situation; Rodney King controlled that. The
suspect always controls the use of force."

The suspect always controls the use of force. Bobby
Leaks in Newark would certainly agree, as would the cops
who stopped Jonny Gammage, as would Hubbard and Pena.
Each claims their behavior was merely a reaction (and in
keeping with police policy) to the behavior of the suspects
they were facing. The Gammage cops all said the suspect was
confrontational and ignored their commands. Nevers and
Budzyn said they repeatedly ordered Malice Green to drop
whatever was in his hand; he refused. Hubbard painfully
recounted how he three times ordered a suspect to drop his

knife before pulling the trigger. Leaks fired his service revolver only when his life was threatened, after the suspect climbed over the seat of his police car, started its engine, and took off with the officer hanging halfway out of the car. Pena's response came after the lives of two fellow officers were threatened.

**Change of venue.** After the four Rodney King cops won a change of venue, and, subsequently, the case—none were convicted—prosecutors began fighting change of venue motions tooth and nail. No district attorney wanted charges that they had blown the case by allowing a white, suburban jury to determine the guilt or innocence of cops who dealt with a racially diverse population. This often ignores massive, negative pretrial publicity against the officers, much of it from local politicians looking to push up approval ratings in the wake of a tragedy. Pena couldn't get a change of venue; neither could Nevers or Budzyn, although the mayor of Detroit had already pronounced them guilty. Prosecutors fought against a change of venue in the Gammage case but lost; a jury pool from outside Pittsburgh was imported. The more dispassionate pool acquitted Vojtas.

**Politics.** Police commissioners are appointed by mayors, and mayors are elected by the general population. When any portion of that population demands action, the political future of both is suddenly at stake. Rather than the typical investigation, suddenly there is tremendous pressure to—as Johnnie Cochran so memorably argued—rush to judgment. In the Rodney King case, in the Nevers/Budzyn case, and in the Leaks case, the mayors of all three cities publicly spurned the officers to appease local activists. Newark's Sharpe James did so despite an ongoing investigation into one of the most vocal groups of demonstrators, an alleged drug-dealing gang called the Zoo Crew. CNN's live shots of Los Angeles burning were not anything that any elected official anywhere wanted repeated.

There was another similarity: every officer was second-guessed, third-guessed, fourth-guessed—often by people who ignored the facts, or twisted the facts, or never wanted to hear the facts in the first place. These are stories of what happens when the second-guessing begins. And when it's over, when the second-guessing stops, there's always one question that hangs heavy over each officer.

It was best posed by former U.S. Labor Secretary Raymond Donovan, who was tried in the Bronx on corruption charges. He was acquitted, but only after months of public humiliation and ridicule. As he left the courthouse, he asked a simple question:

"Which office do I go to to get my reputation back?"

No one offered an answer. He's not alone in waiting to hear a reply.

*Chapter 2*

# THE ZAHREY CASE:

## *POLICE POLITICS MAKE STRANGE DEFENDANTS*

**THE POLICE TOW POUND** in Brooklyn is a dank, depressing spot: a jailhouse for cars, surrounded by a fence and barbed wire. It is not where Zaher Zahrey—a detective known to all in the Brooklyn South Narcotics Unit as Zack—figured on marking his twelfth anniversary as one of New York's Finest.

But five days a week, the pound is now Zahrey's beat—a kind of law enforcement limbo as he awaits final resolution of a case that began in March 1994, when the detective was earning plaudits for his fearless work as an undercover narcotics cop, literally putting his life on the line every day after he kissed his wife and kids goodbye.

Until that March evening, when an Internal Affairs Bureau detective received a phone call from a confidential informant, Zahrey was regarded as a role model for younger cops in the department. His reputation was certainly better than that of the informant, who had a criminal record. The snitch had also been drinking that day. But he had a story to

peddle: Zahrey, he said, was a member of a murderous, rene-
gade Brooklyn street gang known as the Supreme Crew.

The crew was well known to investigators. They were
renowned for their quick and brutal crimes, most often rip-
ping off drug dealers for their stash and cash—crimes that
were lucrative and generally went unreported. They had one
bigger score, though: a March 1992 armored car robbery that
netted $186,000.

During the heist, the Supreme Crew shot and killed a
seventy-one-year-old armored car
guard. A prosecutor would later
charge that William Rivera—an erst-
while friend of Zahrey who allegedly
turned to crime—was "tickled pink"
when he read about the rip-off the
next day in the Daily News. The dead
man's daughter would weep in a
courtroom five years later when a prosecutor described the
heinous crime.

**Before there were any trials—and there would be three—the charges against the three cops would change.**

As for Rivera, he never heard the prosecutor's words or
saw the daughter's tears. He too was dead, gunned down
while partying in a Brooklyn disco. The murder weapon,
improbably, belonged to an off-duty police officer. It was
Rivera's murder that started the chain of events that led to
the phone call and the case against his childhood friend,
Detective Zahrey.

Corrupt cops had become an obsession of the new
administration at City Hall in the wake of stunning admis-
sions by rogue officers during the public Mollen Commission
hearings, which were chaired by a former judge. The police

Internal Affairs Office was given more money, more staff, and a new mandate: get aggressive in rooting out corrupt cops. The police Internal Affairs Office was upgraded to a bureau, with its manpower and budget both significantly increased. Another watchdog group was created: the Mayor's Commission on Police Corruption.

"You could be certain that there was increased pressure that information of corruption be brought to the surface and investigated," acknowledged former Internal Affairs Bureau chief John Mack. He wasn't talking specifically about one case, but his message was clear. That one, brief phone call turned Detective Zahrey's life upside-down. Authorities had trouble making a case against Zahrey until they offered a deal to a career criminal and crackhead looking to beat a potential life sentence—a man who was Zahrey's antithesis, but whose word they would accept over the young detective's.

**"Why stick out your neck? If you don't get involved, the pay is the same. Why take the chance of getting prosecuted, sued, losing your job?"**

Three years later, when he finally landed on his feet with his name and reputation cleared by a federal jury, Zahrey received his new assignment: the Brooklyn tow pound.

Zack Zahrey's life had followed a Hollywood-like script: son of immigrants makes good in the biggest city in the United States. And Zahrey, in a way that surprised even himself, made very good.

His parents moved to Brooklyn from their native Palestine, settling into the relatively sedate Sunset Park section. They opened a family grocery store where Zahrey and his sisters pitched in to help; on his days off, Zahrey traded his police blues for a white apron.

Zahrey became assimilated into the local culture, developing a deep devotion for the city game: basketball. It was a somewhat unrequited love; although he grew to 6-foot-2, Zack didn't make the cut for the Fort Hamilton High School team.

But he befriended the team's best player, William "Supreme" Rivera, a playground legend who dominated the neighborhood courts at 56th Street. Zahrey's game improved from sharing the court with the talented Supreme. Both became well known to the trash-talkers and NBA-wannabes who populated the local courts. Later, their paths diverged.

**Bang! Bang! Blake Hubbard's life had just changed forever, by forces over which he had zero control. Hubbard was on his way to a law-enforcement version of *The Twilight Zone*, where nothing seemed as it appeared.**

Zahrey went to college, but he quickly lost interest in his studies, and his grades tumbled. He was looking for something that could inspire him the way basketball did, and he felt himself drawn to police work.

"I just decided it was something to do—a challenge," Zahrey says. The young man who as a kid had never wanted to be a cop was sworn onto the force on July 8, 1985.

As he had on the court, Zahrey proved to be a quick learner. He worked in his native borough and posed for photos with Mayor Edward I. Koch when the city official stopped by the precinct house. Between 1988 and 1991, he earned seven commendations for excellent police duty.

Zahrey became totally absorbed with his work.

"Oh, I really, really loved the job," he said later. "The guys. The rapport. I had nothing negative to say about the department."

His home life was just as good. Zahrey married a beautiful woman in 1989. Four fellow officers provided a police honor guard for the new couple, who marched beneath their crossed swords. The Zahreys had three children, one after the other: girl, boy, girl.

The walk, talk, and attitude Zack honed on the basketball courts translated into law enforcement success. He began working undercover, handling ultra-dangerous buy-and-bust assignments in notoriously bad neighborhoods. And his superiors hailed him in a 1991 evaluation as a team player willing to share information with fellow officers and help break in new cops. He thrived under difficult conditions.

"I was really into my undercover work," he said. "Risking my life in the roughest, toughest neighborhoods in Brooklyn.... You pick up things playing basketball that you can use [like] 'in your face.' You pick up the slang and the words. Plus I was born and raised in Brooklyn."

In one fifteen-month stretch, Zahrey pulled off 131 undercover drug buys. His chameleonic ability to create new looks and personas increased his value and was appreciated by his bosses.

"Officer Zahrey is highly effective in his role," enthused his supervisor, Lt. James O'Donnell. "He is able to perform well under conditions which are as often as not extremely hazardous."

The August 8, 1992, evaluation ended with a single sentence: "P.O. Zahrey is recommended for promotion to detective investigator."

Three months later, less than eight years after joining the NYPD, Zahrey collected his detective's shield from Police Commissioner Raymond W. Kelly in a ceremony at One Police Plaza.

Once promoted, Zahrey continued his stellar work. A May 15, 1993, performance evaluation said the newly minted detective "is innovative and perseverant... a leader among his peers... this undercover officer exemplifies the undercover officer."

In the last police evaluation before his arrest, Zahrey was hailed as "an asset to the department. He shows excellent judgment, innovativeness, and pride in every task.... He continually shows above standard levels in every assignment."

That was December 1995. Ten months later, he was arraigned inside the same courthouse where he once pulled security duty during the 1986 trial of the nation's No. 1 mob boss, Gambino family head John Gotti. Shortly thereafter, he was jailed in the same building—the Manhattan Correctional Center—where the Dapper Don did time between court appearances.

While Zahrey was working his way through the ranks of the department, Officer Michael Dowd was compiling some impressive—if diametrically opposite—statistics of his own.

Dowd joined the NYPD in 1982 and quickly learned how to line his own pockets by misusing his gun and badge. Making as much as $4,000 a week in protection money paid by drug dealers, Dowd drove a sports car, took exotic vacations, owned four homes, and snorted lines of cocaine off the dashboard of his patrol car.

He was more than just a solo act, though. Dowd organized other cops into crews that robbed drug dens in order to seize drugs and cash. Dowd would return to his suburban Long Island home and peddle the dope to his neighbors for their recreational use, a weekend snort after mowing the lawn.

Dowd also admitted cutting a deal with a drug dealer that was shocking even by the rogue cop's standards. To settle a debt, the veteran cop was going to kidnap a woman and turn her over to Colombian drug dealers for execution.

It was tawdry. It was stunning. It was repulsive. And it was all live on television in 1993, when Dowd was one of the star witnesses before the Mollen Commission, a mayoral panel probing the city's biggest police scandal in two decades. Such tales did little for the reelection hopes of Mayor David Dinkins, who was subsequently defeated by former prosecutor Rudolph Giuliani's law-and-order campaign.

When Dowd went public, spinning his horrid tales on the nightly news, police corruption was catapulted to a level of public concern unseen since Frank Serpico's salad days. Virtually one full shift at a Manhattan police precinct— dubbed "The Dirty Thirty"—was implicated in an operation similar to the one run by the Dowd gang.

On September 8, 1993, Sergeant Robert Boyce was transferred to the Internal Affairs Bureau (IAB) as part of its increased staff. Boyce, an eleven-year police veteran with seventy departmental citations, was investigating a murder committed with a police officer's gun in March 1994 when he and Zahrey first met inside the Sixty-seventh Precinct.

Zahrey's friendship with "Supreme" Rivera had tailed off about the time that the officer was transferred to the Brooklyn South Narcotics Unit in 1991. He was no longer working in and around Sunset Park; and Rivera, according to authorities, had moved into a life of crime.

The pair would sometimes still cross paths on the courts at 56th Street, where both would come for a respite from their different and deadly worlds. It was during one of those pick-up games, during a break in the action, that Supreme introduced Zack to another player: Sidney "Bubba" Quick.

It was a meeting that would have tremendous repercussions for everyone involved. It was also May 1993, the same month as Zahrey's glowing department appraisal.

Quick, now thirty-one, was a stone drug addict whose crack habit imperiled every purse in Brooklyn. He played basketball between robberies, but spent much more time on the latter. He kept his gun courtside. While Zahrey was lean and lithe, Quick had the bulky body of a power forward— Charles Barkley, as opposed to Zack's Grant Hill.

Bubba Quick started using drugs at age thirteen. He alternately abused marijuana, cocaine, heroin, and crack. Plagued by his drug woes, Quick was never able to land any job better than a laborer—and was never able to hold one for more than four months. He received his high school equivalency diploma while in jail. For a brief time, Quick was a crack dealer—but he showed little aptitude for that job, either, and soon lost it, too.

When he was sixteen, Quick began his life of crime by stealing a car. He quickly turned to street crime—muggings, purse snatchings, anything to make some quick cash that could be converted into something to snort, smoke, or shoot.

He did ninety days on Riker's Island for grand larceny in 1982, and six months there in 1984 for another robbery. In January 1985 he received a three- to ten-year term after pleading guilty to seven purse snatchings and robberies. After getting out in May 1989, he was back in jail for another purse snatching in November 1989. Bubba received a two- to five-year bid on that charge, which kept him behind bars until 1993.

He was a well-known figure to the local cops, but not to Zahrey.

"Who knows what these guys in the park do?" he said. "I go there, play a game of pick-up basketball, and I leave. I never said, 'Bubba, let's go get a beer. Let's go to your house.' I never done that with anybody."

Quick was considerably friendlier with Supreme Rivera. After getting out of jail in April 1993, he joined the Supreme Crew and financed his dope habit with drugs and cash seized at gunpoint from drug dealers in and around Sunset Park. The crew members were not his co-conspirators, he would say later; they were his friends dating back to the early eighties—the same time that Quick opted to become a street criminal.

Quick's friendship with Rivera came to a sudden and brutal end on March 10, 1994. Supreme was in a Brooklyn disco when he was shot to death. Another reveler had seized a weapon from the waistband of an off-duty cop inside the club, and emptied it into Supreme. Sixteen shots were fired; fourteen found their target.

The leader of the Supreme Crew was dead.

Bubba Quick received the news while in prison.

Zack Zahrey received the news from Supreme's mother. Could he please go over to the police precinct and find out what had happened to her son? Zahrey had worked the night before; he was tired. But he agreed to do a favor for his late friend's mom.

No good deed ever goes unpunished, the old joke goes. Zahrey didn't laugh when he discovered the truth behind the gag.

On the night of Supreme's death, Sergeant Boyce of the IAB was trying to figure out how a cop's gun was used to kill a local thug. As Boyce was speaking with people inside the precinct, Zahrey showed up to see what he could find out for the Rivera family.

Something about Zahrey's behavior set off Boyce's radar. "Mr. Zahrey was, appeared to be, in an agitated state," Boyce later recalled. "He continually told me that he had nothing to do with these people... and that family members had approached him and asked him to come in and ask about the case."

Despite his initial apprehension, Boyce asked Zahrey—who acknowledged knowing Rivera—if Zahrey could ask around to see what the word on the street was about Supreme's death. Zahrey agreed. Early investigation had indicated that someone known only as "Gucci" was involved, and Zahrey was asked to dig up anything he could on this suspect.

"He gave me his card: 'Anything comes up—anything— you give me a call. I'm asking you to help me out,'" Zahrey recalled of their conversation.

Four days later, Zahrey agreed to meet with Boyce at the Bridgeview Diner in Brooklyn's Bay Ridge section. Zahrey came directly from Supreme's funeral, and spent an hour speaking with Boyce and another investigator.

Over a cup of coffee, Zahrey shared what he had learned with the two cops. According to the undercover narcotics detective, the cop involved was dirty—his family was in the drug business. The cop was providing security for the drug dealer, the man who actually pulled the trigger, and he had allowed the dealer to use his weapon in the hit on Rivera.

Zahrey had more. He provided the names of three pur- ported eyewitnesses to the slaying. And he suggested a nearby Bay Ridge bar where the cop and the drug dealer were known to hang out—the Flipside.

Boyce took down the information. But his bad feelings about Zahrey—despite the detective's obvious cooperation in the Supreme murder—didn't go away.

Nine days later, the IAB received a phone call from an informant. A police report noted that the man was "quite intoxicated" and "rambled on"; he invited investigators to meet him at a bar. The informant had been arrested in 1988 for possession of a hand grenade—an item he had inexplicably brought to a police funeral. The informant had an axe to grind as well; his daughter's fiancée had allegedly been murdered by Zahrey's friend, "Supreme" Rivera.

But his story grabbed the attention of everyone at the IAB: Zahrey was helping a gang rob drug dealers. And Zahrey had actually attended the murder of a rival drug dealer. This was exactly the kind of case that the new IAB wanted to make.

After this phone call, Boyce "opened a log"—he officially began an Internal Affairs investigation of Detective Zahrey, based on that one phone call from one drunken informant. A spotless nine-year career was ignored.

Zahrey had gone from the hunter to the game.

Boyce turned up zero in his investigation for five months—until he paid a jailhouse visit to Bubba Quick. The first visit was fruitless. The second visit was the same. But on his third trip to see Bubba Quick in the infamous Sing Sing Prison, Boyce persuaded Quick to cooperate.

How he did it was another story.

When Boyce arrived at the prison in March 1995, Quick was approaching his thirtieth birthday with a likely life sentence as a persistent, violent felon to mark the occasion. The prospect of spending the rest of his sorry life behind bars appeared to jog Quick's memory.

So did some harsh rhetoric from Boyce.

Boyce asked about the October 1993 murder of a Brooklyn drug dealer named J. R. Guadalupe. "I didn't have nothing to do with this... 'Member, I was cracked out when this happened," Quick initially responded.

Boyce wasn't satisfied. He held out a carrot for Bubba.

"[If] you can put Zack as part of that killing, part of that shooting, that murder, you would get a very, very, very sweet deal," Boyce promised during the interview, which was taped and later transcribed as evidence. "You understand what I'm saying?"

Zahrey didn't deserve to wear the same badge as he, Boyce fumed. He needed Quick's help to "nail Zack to the cross." And if Quick could provide that help, Boyce told him, "I'll drive you home"—a get-out-of-jail free pass.

"The deal," Boyce said bluntly, "is Zack. That's what your deal is. You understand that?"

Bubba Quick's memory suddenly improved.

He implicated Zahrey in the Guadalupe murder, saying the detective had helped Rivera dispose of the murder weapon in the East River. He remembered plenty of other evil deeds done by Zahrey, too—his ability to target drug spots for robberies based on police intelligence. Or the time Zahrey provided fake badges and police jackets for a robbery. He remembered Zahrey taking his cut of cocaine and cash after another heist. He remembered Zahrey selling handguns out of the trunk of his car.

His memory jogged futher, Quick recalled that, yes, now that he thought about it, Zahrey was a very, very, very dirty cop. And Bubba was, as Boyce promised, looking at a very, very, very sweet deal indeed.

Quick signed a cooperation agreement, and his life sentence was suddenly a ten-year maximum, with a good shot at parole because of his efforts to help convict Zahrey. Assistant District Attorney Theresa Corrigan, in a phone call that

Quick placed from prison, assured the star witness that it was unlikely he would ever do ten years.

"The worst that can happen to you under the cooperation agreement is that ten years," she assured him when Quick called from jail, a conversation that was taped. "That's it. That's the worst. And the only way you're gonna look at ten years is you totally start lying... stop being helpful to us and beneficial to us."

Corrigan's office initially handled the Zahrey investigation, but that caused a serious problem. Under New York State law, uncorroborated accomplice testimony is insufficient for a conviction. And that was all they had on Zahrey: the word of Bubba Quick.

But the prosecutors came up with a simple solution: They transferred the case into federal court, where the rules were different. Quick would be enough for a conviction in the U.S. District Court in Brooklyn.

That decision didn't stop investigators from trying other tactics as well to bring Zahrey down. Two alleged members of the Supreme Crew were taken by police investigators to secret locations—one to a Queens warehouse, the other to a Staten Island hotel—and questioned for hours without their lawyers. The investigators wanted to know all about Zahrey.

"There was no doubt they wanted a cop," said Frank Geoly, attorney for one of the pair. But neither was able to provide police with anything to incriminate Zahrey.

Boyce then tried to use Quick as a conduit for Zahrey to incriminate himself. On September 6, 1994, Quick was brought into the Brooklyn district attorney's office to contact

Zahrey. The career criminal called the cop's beeper number and punched in the number of a confidential telephone line in the prosecutor's office.

Quick tried repeatedly to draw some admission out of Zahrey, some acknowledgement of their mutual life of crime. He failed.

"You know what the fuck I do?" Quick asked. "You know what the fuck we do?"

"No, no, no, no, no, no, no, no, no, no," Zahrey said. "…I don't know nothing about that shit. Nothing."

At another point in the conversation, Zahrey flatly tells Quick that "I never did nothing, so I'm not down with that shit."

Near the end of their talk, Zahrey gave Bubba a bit of philosophical advice: "Just a little time changes a lot of things. You think right now things are hot for you, things are fucked up for you, but believe me—things, and a little time, and a lot of shit changes."

Zahrey didn't know it, but he would soon need to follow that advice himself.

On August 10, 1995, Zahrey's NYPD assignment was "modified." While in the field, members of the IAB approached him and took his shield and his gun. The highly praised undercover narcotics detective was reassigned to clerical duty in a Manhattan courthouse.

Zahrey was stunned. He thought that a fellow cop—the brother of the officer involved in the Rivera shooting—had decided to paint him as dirty, a payback for his cooperation in the murder investigation. He never thought to ask about Bubba Quick—not that he would have received an answer.

"They refused to answer any questions," Zahrey said. "They said it was a criminal investigation of serious gravity, and that we can't tell you nothing. We're here for your gun and your badge."

Zahrey remained in administrative limbo while prosecutors worked on improving their case. But they found no more witnesses to back up Quick, and so they brought the case to a federal grand jury with their single, tainted witness. The grand jury returned an indictment.

On October 16, 1996, the handcuffs that once dangled from Zahrey's belt were placed around his own wrists. Detective Zaher Zahrey, NYPD, was charged in the murder of J. R. Guadalupe. He was accused of a conspiracy to distribute cocaine. He was charged with firearms trafficking, and with failing to turn in his co-conspirators.

Zahrey was suspended from the police force. The distraught cop, off the job and facing federal charges, had one thing going for him: his family. He had their shoulders to cry on, their attention when he wanted to vent his frustration. They were a constant, supportive presence. And then he lost that, too.

On November 7, 1996, prosecutors went before U.S. District Court Judge Nina Gershon with a tale told by Bubba Quick's mother, Hannah. According to Mrs. Quick, she had received a phone call threatening her life. The caller, she said, spoke two sentences: "I'm Zack Zahrey. You're dead." The detective, who had been released on $500,000 bail after two family members put up their houses for collateral, had met Mrs. Quick just once—a twenty-second encounter nearly three years earlier.

Mrs. Quick said she was certain the voice on the phone was Zahrey's. Judge Gershon believed Bubba's mother, and she revoked Zahrey's bail.

For the next six months, Zahrey was locked up in Manhattan's Metropolitan Correctional Center, held in solitary confinement for his own protection—just one more bit of hell for accused cops to handle. He was allowed only three hours of family visits and a single personal phone call per week. His wife of eight years and their three children became a vague memory. His wife lied to the children, not wanting them to know that dad had swapped his police uniform for an orange prison jump suit. But Zahrey felt the older kids knew the ugly truth. And that was the worst of all, he recalled.

"That was the low point for me," Zahrey said. "It broke my heart with my family. The lowest point for me, physically and emotionally, was the day the judge affirmed my bail revocation."

Zahrey left his prison cell on May 8, 1997, and headed for his day in court. His attorney, Joel Rudin, told the jury in his opening statement that, yes, Zahrey knew Supreme Rivera and had met Bubba Quick. But that, the lawyer said, did not make him a dirty cop.

"You can't turn your back on the people you grew up with and played ball with," Rudin said. Rivera and Zahrey were lifelong pals, basketball buddies, partners in a failed construction business. They were not partners in crime, he insisted.

The courtroom was sparsely populated, with the exception of the first row behind the defense table. Zahrey's wife, parents, and siblings filled those seats every day. An occasional reporter stopped by the proceedings, but Zahrey's battle for the return of his badge was little more than a blip on the media's radar screen in the Big Apple.

The hulking Bubba Quick, wearing his blue prison-issue uniform, his dreadlocks tied back in a ponytail, arrived to tell his story to the jury on May 21. Assistant U.S. Attorney Martin Coffey asked Quick how his testimony could affect his jail sentence.

"Do you know what the maximum sentence is you could get?" Coffey inquired.

"Ten years," Quick answered.

"Do you know what the minimum or lowest sentence is you could get?"

"Nothing," said Bubba Quick.

The first forty minutes of his testimony were devoted to running down his life of crime, his problems behind bars, his drug use. At one point, Quick discussed his 1992 stay at the Shawangunk Correctional Facility. After the witness garbled the pronunciation, Coffey asked, "Can you spell that?"

"No," Quick replied.

Quick then filled the fourth-floor courtroom with his tales of Zahrey as a corrupt cop, a criminal much worse than many of the people currently incarcerated with Bubba.

As Quick repeatedly implicated Zahrey, the accused cop furiously scribbled notes on a legal pad. He sat silently, blinking his eyes in stunned disbelief, as Quick rambled on and on. At one point, when Quick testified that Zahrey had set the gang up with stolen police shields, the detective angrily shook his head—no, no, no, no, no—and slam-dunked a Life Saver candy into his mouth. Rudin sat anxiously beside him at the defense table, chomping at the bit for his shot at Quick.

When it finally came, Rudin made the most of it.

Rudin's three-day cross-examination of Quick was devastating and, at some points, comical. Quick had testified under questioning from the prosecution that while running from police, he hung off an apartment building rooftop and jumped through a window in an effort to escape. Rudin, early in his cross-examination, asked Quick how he felt after smoking crack.

"I never tried to fly or jump off no roof," Quick replied. "I was aware of my surroundings when I was high."

Rudin shot back, "Didn't you testify on direct examination that you did jump off a roof through a window?"

"I didn't actually jump off the roof," Quick corrected the lawyer. "I jumped inside."

Rudin exposed inconsistencies in Quick's stories, contradictions in the facts, holes large enough to drive trucks through.

Quick testified, for example, that he and Zahrey had robbed a dope dealer in a Brooklyn park. In a session with Boyce, Quick said the hold-up took place in winter 1992. Unfortunately, Quick was behind bars at that time.

On the evening of the J. R. Guadalupe shooting, Quick said, he and Supreme Rivera met with Zahrey at 6:30 PM. A police log showed that Zahrey didn't sign out of work until 7 PM. And while Quick insisted that the white-skinned Zahrey stood and watched as Rivera gunned down Guadalupe, another eyewitness had testified the killer was a dark-skinned black man.

According to Quick's testimony, the only dark-skinned black man at the scene that night was Bubba Quick. Rudin later argued that the government, in its zeal to bag Zahrey, had given Quick a walk on the slaying.

"If you had said that you pulled the trigger, you wouldn't have gotten the deal, right?" Rudin asked Quick at the end of his questioning.

Quick never answered. A prosecution objection was sustained before the hulking inmate could open his mouth.

With that, Sidney "Bubba" Quick completed his career as a federal witness.

Although Quick had alleged that Zahrey helped rob drug dealers, sold illegal handguns, and collected $200,000 as his cut of the Supreme Crew's booty, corroborating evidence was nil. There were no eyewitnesses to put Zahrey at crime scenes. No incriminating physical evidence—fingerprints, phone records, cash—was ever recovered. And police surveillance of Zahrey found him doing nothing more venal than working in the family store in his white apron.

Rudin called a pair of witnesses who knew both Zahrey and Supreme Rivera. Richard Del Rio, pastor of the Abounding Grace Christian Center, knew Zahrey as a fellow basketball aficionado. Del Rio, who conducted Rivera's funeral, recalled that friends of the late Supreme were bent on revenge following the service. And it was Zahrey who managed to defuse the angry situation.

"He certainly wasn't fueling the fire there," Del Rio testified. "He assured them that he would be able to take care of it. You know, that we will take care of it.... He intimated that the police would take care of it."

Zahrey's last line of defense was his lawyer, Rudin, who delivered an impassioned summation. The jury sat, listening intently, as Rudin described Zahrey as a victim of politics far removed from the Brooklyn streets where he made his living. His arrest and trial had forever changed Zahrey's life for the worse.

"Something surely has died in Detective Zahrey as a result of this case," Rudin said in his closing argument. "He gave eleven of the best years of his life to this city. He voluntarily took on the most dangerous job known to the police department, the undercover narcotics detective, going to highly dangerous locations with no backup, knowing that he could be dead before anyone even knew that he was in trouble... only to have his reputation, his career, his life shattered, based upon the word of a totally unreliable predator-crackhead."

Why?

"So that the Internal Affairs Bureau, the Brooklyn district attorney's office, and the United States attorney's office could justify their involvement in a fruitless two-year investigation while making it look like they were doing something to fight police corruption," Rudin argued.

In his final words to the jury, Rudin delivered a powerful message.

"Do not let them get away with this shameful, disgraceful case. If you let them destroy Detective Zahrey, if Sidney Quick's word is enough evidence to convict a New York City police detective, then 'do not send to know for whom the bell tolls,'" Rudin said, quoting the English poet John Donne. "'It tolls for thee.'"

"They have not proven Detective Zahrey guilty of any of the hateful, despicable crimes charged in the indictment. Give him back his life. Give him back his dignity.

"He is not guilty."

The jury went out to deliberate on June 27, 1996. They took a quick vote on Zahrey's innocence or guilt. They reached their decision, one juror said later, in less than five minutes.

"When they said they had a verdict, my stomach was in knots," Zahrey said. "I'm not gonna lie to you. For them, if they got me on one count, it was a victory for them."

They lost.

All twelve jurors agreed; Zahrey was not guilty of anything. The panel never needed a second vote. Afterward, several expressed disgust that the case had ever come to trial.

The prosecution's case "was nonexistent," said juror Karen Rubin. "He wasn't not guilty. He was innocent."

Zahrey walked out of the courthouse a free man, reunited with his family. He went out for a slice of Brooklyn pizza— his first nonjailhouse meal in eight months. He eventually returned to the job—and was assigned to the tow pound.

The police brass didn't welcome him with open arms. "We are reviewing the detective's case, and he is facing departmental charges," said Marilyn Mode, spokeswoman for Police Commissioner Howard Safir. The departmental charges mirrored exactly the accusations that the jury had determined were not committed by the detective.

Mode declined to comment further. But one law enforcement source said that authorities had been aware going in that their case against Zahrey was paper-thin; but they were convinced he had done something wrong, and felt they should prosecute him anyway.

Bill Muller, a spokesman for the U.S. attorney's office, said only, "We stand by the prosecution, and we accept the verdict." No one offered any sympathy for Zahrey, who won the war but lost eight months of his life, and then some.

Zahrey, speaking after the verdict, described Boyce and the rest of IAB as "a combination of the Gestapo and the Keystone Kops." He doesn't like the tow pound, but says he can never return to undercover work because he fears retaliation à la Frank Serpico. Serpico, the whistleblowing cop whose life later became a movie starring Al Pacino, was shot on the job after testifying against crooked cops. Serpico has long questioned whether he was set up by fellow officers as a payback for his decision to expose police corruption.

"I wouldn't want to go out on the street," he said. "I've already been through the fight of my life."

At a news conference in his lawyer's office, Zahrey patiently answered questions from reporters. When it was over, he pulled out a T-shirt and displayed it for the cameras, saying it was a gift from a fellow cop. On the front of the white shirt, in stark black ink, was a police officer flanked by a pair of weapon-toting bad guys. The picture's caption was six words:

"WHO'S NEXT? THIS COULD BE YOU!!"

*Chapter 3*

# THE NEVERS AND BUDZYN CASE

## *THE MAYOR SAYS THEY'RE MURDERERS*

**COLEMAN YOUNG,** the mayor of the city of Detroit, did not wait for a judge or a jury. He did not wait for an investigation. He did not waste any time on constitutional rights, or worries about prejudicing the jury pool, or any of those other legal niceties guaranteed to even the lowest of low-life criminals.

Right there, on national television, Coleman Young looked into a camera and announced that Officers Larry Nevers and Walter Budzyn were guilty of killing one of his fair city's residents. The officers were white. The resident was black.

"A young man who was under arrest was literally murdered by police," Young told television viewers from coast to coast. At the time, Nevers and Budzyn—two veteran cops who were joined as partners for the first time just a month earlier—had not been accused of any crime at all stemming from their November 5, 1992, arrest of a drug suspect in a high-crime Detroit neighborhood.

That—and everything else in the lives of Nevers and Budzyn—changed awfully quickly.

The two were subsequently accused and tried for murder after what had been a routine drug bust gone bad outside a boarded-up hair salon now operating as a crack house. Five of their colleagues were implicated, too, including a black supervisor. All were immediately suspended from the department; four, including Nevers and Budzyn, were fired within six weeks, without any due process.

**The mayor of Detroit didn't wait for a judge or a jury. He didn't waste time on constitutional rights. Instead he announced on national television that the officers were guilty of murder.**

The two cops first met Malice Green, thirty-five, the unemployed father of two, at the intersection of Warren and 23rd streets, on a November evening in 1992. Green had just dropped off a friend near the crackhouse when the officers arrived in their "power unit"—an unmarked police car assigned to patrol high-crime areas. This neighborhood certainly qualified. These blocks had helped Detroit achieve the highest murder rate among major U.S. cities in 1986 and 1987, and to remain near the top of the list five years later.

The police car held a couple of decorated cops. Nevers had spent twenty-four years on the Detroit Police Department, five more than his partner, and had been cited by the Michigan Association of Chiefs of Police for his outstanding work. His aggressive style of police work earned him the street alias of Starsky, after the savvy television cop played by Paul Michael Glaser in Starsky and Hutch.

Then there was Budzyn. In 1990, he was named Officer of the Year in his precinct for making thirty-one arrests and recovering a half-dozen stolen cars. During his time on the force, he had received one departmental reprimand—for leaving his post without permission to drive an elderly couple into Canada after their car was stolen at a Detroit Tigers game. This pair of formidable forces put Malice Green in their sights.

Green was driving a car pock-marked with bullet holes when he stopped in front of the crackhouse to let a friend out. Earlier that evening, he and the friend—along with some other acquaintances—had been smoking cocaine in a nearby apartment.

Later—five years later—Nevers would look back on this night and consider the scene: The bullet holes. The crackhouse. The sight of Robert Knox, a man he had arrested twice before, leaving the car. "At first glance," he reflected, "this seemed like a prudent stop to me."

When it was over, when the incident at Warren and 23rd had ended a few minutes later, Malice Green was dead, and the two cops—along with their five coworkers—were in deep, deep trouble.

The biggest problem, it seemed, centered on the races of the officers and the dead man. And although the officers worked in Detroit, it was an arrest in California one year earlier that affected much of what happened to them. The specter of Rodney King rose high above the Detroit skyline throughout this case.

The fallout from the 1991 King incident, with the subsequent rioting after the officers involved were acquitted in

April 1992, had city officials around the country on edge. Forty-four people had been killed, two thousand more wounded, and $1 billion in damage was wrought before that nightmare in Los Angeles was brought under control.

No elected official wanted a repeat of the King affair or its violent aftermath. Detroit Mayor Coleman Young, whose city had burned during the riots of the late 1960s, certainly wanted no repeat of those ugly days under his regime. And so, four days after Malice Green died, Young offered up the heads of his cops as a peace offering.

That solved nothing. Indeed, in many ways, Young's comments created more problems in a case that was to polarize his city and rattle his police department. Lawsuits brought by Nevers and Budzyn's backup (also accused) on the night of the death cost the city millions in settlement money. Nevers and Budzyn were convicted of murder, but won new trials in 1997 after their appeals exposed bureaucratic bungling during their initial trials. Budzyn, in his retrial, was convicted on a lesser charge of involuntary manslaughter—a verdict he could still appeal. Nevers awaits his second shot before a jury.

Their cases drag on and on and on.

"This case cost the city a lot more than money," attorney David Griem, who represented one of the other accused cops in the case, told the Detroit Free Press in 1997. "It cost the city part of its soul. So many people's lives were adversely impacted by this."

Nevers and Budzyn were released a few months apart in 1997; Nevers hopes his new trial will share the same less racially heightened atmosphere that marked the Budzyn retrial. Both have always, and still do, maintain their innocence. Nevers, in a lengthy posting on an internet site designed to raise funds for his ever-escalating defense bills, went as far as to list a half-dozen crimes committed that night by Green, from resisting arrest to possession of cocaine.

"Below," Nevers continues, "is a list of laws my partner and I broke that same night."

A blank space follows.

There was no early indication that the police stop in the affair of Malice Green would be anything more than one small dance in the endless pas de deux between cops and drug dealers in the city of Detroit. Nevers and Budzyn were on patrol, trying to stick their fingers into the dike of dope flooding the streets of this neighborhood. Nevers, with seventeen years and more than eight thousand man hours spent on the streets there, was likely the most qualified man for such an assignment in the entire Detroit Police Department.

**"These situations simply will not occur if the person about to be arrested simply complies with the orders of the officers involved."**

At about 10:30 PM that fall night, Green pulled over to drop off a friend, Robert Knox, outside a crackhouse near the apartment of another passenger in the car, Ralph Fletcher. Nevers said he initially thought Green's red car had been stolen at gunpoint one night earlier, but he quickly realized it was the wrong make and model. Still, the bullet holes in the front fender piqued his interest. He then spotted Knox, a local druggie, running from the car and toward Fletcher's apartment; the two cops pulled over behind the parked car, with Budzyn going after Knox while Nevers walked over to the car.

Malice Green, a Detroit man who had two kids, no job, and a penchant for smoking cocaine was behind the wheel. He had worked at an Illinois steel mill, a job that fell through ten months before his death. Police in Waukegan, Illinois, had had several run-ins with Green during his time there. His estranged wife was living in North Carolina, and Green would occasionally speak of moving to join her.

But that night, he had opted to smoke cocaine with Fletcher. The two men had been planning on returning to party later on, when they encountered the two cops.

What happened next, as related later by prosecutors to Detroit juries, was simple: The officers asked Green for his driver's license. Green reached into his glove compartment and pulled something out inside a closed hand. The police demanded that Green drop whatever was in his hand, fearing it might be a weapon. Green refused, and the officers repeatedly smashed him in the head with their three-pound police issue flashlights. The officers called for backup; when help arrived, those officers—Robert Lessnau, Karl Gunther, Paul Gotelaere, and James Kijek—either joined in the beating or stood by and watched as the assault on the injured Green continued (more on this later).

Those four officers were white. A fifth officer, who was black, was the supervisor on the scene. He, too, allowed the beating to occur.

The officers then flagged down a passing Emergency Medical Service ambulance to assist the dying man.

This much is not in dispute: Malice Green died on the way to Detroit Receiving Hospital. An autopsy would later show that he had cocaine and alcohol in his system. It would also show that while Green was supposedly smashed in the head at least fourteen times with heavy flashlights wielded by two officers, he suffered no skull fractures—a discovery that later provided fodder for defense attorneys.

Larry Nevers remembered that night a little differently.

He remembered Budzyn asking for Green's license as he, Nevers, "began a light-hearted conversation" with a small group of neighborhood characters standing near the car. One of the group, Robert Hollins, suddenly asked Nevers, "What's with your partner? He's in trouble. You'd better get over there."

Budzyn later testified that after he asked Green to show his driver's license, the suspect had reached toward his glove compartment and emerged with a clenched first. It was impossible, at first, to determine if Green was clutching a weapon, and the suspect refused to open his hand. Budzyn testified that he later discovered Green was clutching rocks of cocaine.

Nevers ran over to the car, where he found Budzyn and Green wrestling in the front seat. Budzyn was ordering the suspect to open his clenched fist. Green ignored him. Green kicked Budzyn in the chest, further wrestling ensued, and Green dropped a rock of cocaine.

Nevers said he struck Green on the hand in an effort to get the suspect to surrender the rest of his stash. "I remember trying to understand why Green was reacting so violently," the officer recalled. "Why was he doing this? What was he hiding?"

The brawling continued, and Nevers said that Green then reached for the weapon in his holster. A decade earlier, Nevers was in a similar situation, where his partner was forced to shoot a suspect who made a move to grab his weapon. Nevers had determined that he would never again let himself get in the same situation. He struck Green with the flashlight, three or four times, until the suspect let go of the gun.

Green's hand then came up holding "a metallic object," and he began swinging at Nevers's head. Nevers responded by hitting him "two or three times on the head with my flashlight." Police backup arrived at the scene and pulled Green out of the car. Police eventually recovered four chunks of cocaine from the scene, and a small pocketknife from one of Green's pockets. It was determined that the shiny object in Green's hand was his keys.

Nevers, five years later, recalled the ensuing events as a "nightmare"—and the nightmare started almost immediately, with Police Chief Stanley Knox getting on television just seventeen hours after the death to suspend the seven officers on the scene. Asked if he could see similarities to the Rodney King case, an emotional Knox replied, "I think we all do."

But he didn't limit his comments to just that damning remark. "This incident is disgraceful and a total embarrassment to all good officers that have worked so hard to make this department one of the best in the nation," Knox said. "...Our investigation shows that seven officers were there, were there and took some part in it, so seven officers are being suspended."

He then offered this parting shot: "We cannot tolerate this kind, this type of officer on this job."

What Knox didn't say was that the press conference was a violation of departmental policy. Under police rules, a departmental board of review has ten days to investigate any case where a suspect was killed by a gun or by force. But Knox decided not to wait. Other top police brass said they encouraged Knox to hold off until the prosecutor decided whether to file charges against the cops and which cops might be charged.

There were other problems with his handling of the officers, other variations from ordinary departmental practice with such cases:

■ No three-member board of review was named to oversee the probe and guarantee its fairness.

■ The suspensions came before the investigation was completed, and all the officers on the scene—regardless of their roles—were lumped together.

■ The officers were not allowed to offer any explanation, and some of the cops did not receive specific allegations of wrongdoing until three months later.

Three days after the suspensions, Mayor Coleman Young convicted his cops unilaterally during an interview with NBC News. He was widely praised for taking quick action to defuse any angry response from the city's mostly black population. But none of that praise came from Nevers or Budzyn, who were flabbergasted by this turn of events.

In contrast to the Green death, a fatal police shooting five months later was handled entirely differently by Detroit's police brass; in this instance, there was less attention paid to the police response and a less racially explosive mix. Two black officers fatally shot a Latino suspect, prompting a huge outcry from the Hispanic community. The officers were not excoriated by the department—or the mayor—and they were eventually acquitted of second-degree murder and reinstated to their jobs.

But not the cops in the Green arrest. On November 16, eleven days after Malice Green died, prosecutors made it official: Nevers and Budzyn were charged with second-degree murder and ordered held on $100,000 bail each. Sgt. Freddie Douglas, the supervisor on the scene, was charged with manslaughter and failure to uphold the law. Officer Robert Lessnau was charged with intent to commit bodily harm. The other officers at the scene—already suspended by Knox, already condemned by Young—were not charged.

One month later, the four accused cops were fired after a chief's hearing. One week later, a judge dismissed the felony charge against Douglas, allowing a misdemeanor count of willful neglect of duty.

The wrongly implicated cops wound up collecting nearly $4 million in settlements and back pay from the city of Detroit for its mishandling of the case. "The lives of these officers were an afterthought," said attorney Fred Gibson, who represented three of the officers against the city.

The Green case, with the inflammatory remarks of Young and Knox, quickly became a cause célèbre. Reporters from around the country flew into Detroit to cover the "next

Rodney King case." Few bothered to note the absence of any evidence indicating that race was a factor in Malice Green's death. No one heard any of the officers involved using racial epithets. Even the prosecutor who brought the charges didn't cite race as a motive: "What was in their minds is hard to tell," was the comment from Wayne County Prosecutor John D. O'Hair.

Knox himself said he did not feel racism was a motive, noting that the 3,800-member police force for the mostly minority city of 1 million was 58 percent black. But the "white cops, black victim" line appeared in virtually every story about the case, creating a picture of Nevers and Budzyn as Klansmen with badges and guns.

Green, in contrast, was viewed by many in the city as a martyr. Hundreds of strangers turned out at a Detroit funeral home to pay their final respects. An impromptu memorial appeared at the corner where he died, with passers-by stopping to see the hallowed spot. A local artist painted a mural of the dead man that stands to this day at the corner of Warren and 23rd streets.

It was in this atmosphere that Budzyn and Nevers would have their day in court, a day when they would literally be fighting for their lives—each potentially facing life in prison. "I don't believe we're going to get a fair trial in Detroit," said defense attorney John Goldpaugh, speaking one day after Nevers and Budzyn were charged. "When you've got the mayor of the city calling them murderers before they've been tried, how can they get a fair trial?"

Goldpaugh's words proved prescient. But it would take five years to prove him right.

The trial of Nevers and Budzyn began on June 3, 1993; Lessnau was a co-defendant. The first two cops would have their fates determined by separate juries; Lessnau had opted to let Judge George Crockett III decide his fate.

In the intervening months, the cops' lawyers had failed to get a change of venue for the highly volatile case to a locale outside Detroit. It didn't help that city officials, in a tacit admission of guilt, had already agreed to pay Green's family $5.25 million to settle a civil law suit.

It quickly became clear that the pretrial publicity was extensive and relentlessly negative toward the defendants. "I read that police brutality killed this man," one prospective juror said on Day One of jury selection. Outside the courthouse, jurors walked past protesters chanting, "No justice, no quiet. We remember the L.A. riot."

It was a less-than-subtle commentary on the likely results of any acquittals for the cops.

When the juries were seated, Budzyn's panel held eleven blacks and one white. The Nevers' jury was comprised of ten blacks and two whites.

During the opening statements, prosecutors presented the case as a simple, brutal assault. "It was simply the exercise of raw power over one human being by others," said prosecutor Doug Baker. "That's what it's going to be all about."

Words were one thing. Evidence was another. And the prosecution's case against the officers had some problems.

Dr. Kalil Jiraki, the Wayne County assistant medical examiner who did the autopsy on Green, blamed fourteen blows to the head "in rapid sequence" for the man's death.

But Jiraki admitted during the trial that he had not waited for toxicology reports before ruling the death a homicide. In his opinion, the doctor said, nothing could have superseded blunt force trauma to the head as the cause of Malice Green's death. Brain damage, he said, had caused Green's heart and lungs to fail. Yet these repeated, fatal blows did not fracture Green's skull.

"The cause of death was obvious," Jiraki told the jury.

Other experts—three, in all—found the cause of death far less obvious. The combination of blows to the head along with cocaine and alcohol had caused Green's death, according to Oakland County pathologist Dr. Ljubisa Dragovic. His autopsy showed no swelling of Green's brain, which contradicted Jiraki's finding for the cause of death.

Without the swelling, Dragovic testified, "that mechanism of death is out. You have to offer another reason to show why this man died." A more likely explanation, Dragovic went on, was that Green suffered a fatal seizure brought on by cocaine, alcohol, and his brawl with the police. Another defense pathologist said there was no swelling of Green's brain, which is essential to a finding of blunt force trauma as the cause of death. A third defense pathologist agreed with those findings.

The discovery of cocaine in Green's system seemed to explain how the thin, 5-foot-10, 145-pound Green could have put up such a furious fight. During their combined four decades on the police force, Nevers and Budzyn had seen how drugs could turn ordinary people extraordinarily violent.

The prosecution's eyewitnesses were less than poster children for a Detroit good citizenship award. Ralph

Fletcher, a childhood friend of Green, testified that his apartment was a floating party spot where cocaine smoking was a staple. On the night of the incident, he acknowledged, he had been drinking beer and wine since early in the afternoon. Fletcher was riding with Green on the night that his friend died.

Fletcher, although he later insisted that Budzyn was at the scene, could not pick the officer out from a police lineup. And he said that he had never seen Budzyn strike Green in the head. His story also had inconsistencies: He had initially said the beating of Green was done with a nightstick, then later amended that to a flashlight. In another instance, he said that Nevers, not Budzyn, was the first officer in the car; at the trial, he flip-flopped the officers' positions.

Fletcher also backed up one important point in the officers' story. He said that eyewitnesses, along with the police, had implored Green to drop whatever was in his hand. Green had refused.

Teresa Pace, a prostitute known on the street as "Redbone," said she was smoking cocaine with Malice Green inside Fletcher's apartment about forty-five minutes before Green's car was stopped by the cops. She insisted at the trial, however, that she was not "high" or in any way impaired when she watched what happened that night. She acknowledged that Green was carrying a rock of cocaine in his hand. And while she thought that Budzyn was smacking Green in the head with his flashlight, she admitted she could not see clearly into the car or see the flashlight hitting Green.

Pace then said that Nevers, in an effort to get Green to drop whatever was in his hand, struck the suspect on the knee with his flashlight. Though she testified that she thought Green was getting smashed in the head, Pace said that she didn't call 911 for help. And she acknowledged spending the month preceding the trial against Nevers and Budzyn in police headquarters because she lacked a stable address.

Pace's boyfriend, Robert Hollins, started his night on November 5 by driving to Ralph Fletcher's house, drinking some beer, and smoking $10 worth of cocaine. He had another beer at his sister's house before heading back to the Fletcher place to smoke some more cocaine. Hollins, too, never saw Budzyn's flashlight strike Green, although he testified that he could hear it making contact. He agreed with Pace's testimony that Nevers hit Green on the knee after demanding that the suspect drop whatever he was holding in his hand.

Another witness, Manuel Brown, admitted he was smoking cocaine in Fletcher's house on the night of the death, making two trips back and forth to get more dope. Nevers had previously arrested Brown; the suspect had gone to jail based on those arrests.

The most damaging testimony against Nevers came from a Detroit medic who arrived on the scene and saw him strike Green four times in the head with the flashlight. The medic painted a gruesome picture of blood pouring from Green's head into a puddle on the street as Nevers battled with the man, the pair hanging half out of the bullet-ridden car.

But Green, who had a portion of his scalp torn from his skull in the brawl, did not bleed to death. And Nevers acknowledged landing four blows to the suspect's head when Green allegedly went for his service revolver.

The defense put Budzyn on the witness stand, and the veteran cop testified that he had never held his flashlight during the encounter with Green. He denied ever striking the suspect, and said he never saw Nevers strike the man either.

His testimony under oath marked the first time that Budzyn had ever spoken publicly about that night. He echoed Nevers's tale of Green fighting with him over a piece of rock cocaine, and Nevers coming to his aid. Prosecutor Kym Worthy grilled Budzyn on cross-examination, asking at one point: "I'm not saying you did, but if you wanted to fashion a story that would encompass what everyone said, you could do that, couldn't you?"

Replied Budzyn, "I'd rather the truth come out of what happened."

Lessnau followed him to the stand, denying that he had dragged an already injured Green out of the car and into the street for a further assault. When he arrived, Lessnau said, it was clear that Green and Nevers were involved in a knock-down, drag-out fight.

"It looked like Officer Nevers did need assistance," he testified. "…The man appeared to be pulling away." Minutes later, as Nevers tried to get Green out of the car, the bleeding man tried to hold onto the steering wheel with his feet while reaching for a pocketknife in his right pocket, Lessnau said.

Last on the witness stand was Nevers, who told the tale of a shooting incident one decade earlier with another suspect. "I was afraid that he would get my gun out and possibly use it against me or my partner," Nevers said. He acknowledged striking Green in the head, but only in self-defense.

The trial was winding down, with testimony almost over, when the jurors, taking a break, sat down to see a movie selected by a court representative. With closing arguments less than a week away, the jurors were shown Spike Lee's film Malcolm X, a biography of the slain 1960's activist.

Lee's film included a lengthy portion of an amateur video showing Rodney King's beating by police in Los Angeles after a high-speed chase. It also featured an inflammatory voiceover by acclaimed actor Denzel Washington, who portrayed Malcolm X. Washington intoning, "Brothers and sisters, I am here to tell you that I charge the white man with being the greatest murderer on earth.... We didn't see any democracy on the streets of Detroit.... No, we've never seen democracy. All we've seen is hypocrisy. We don't see any American dream. We've experienced only the American nightmare."

Defense attorneys found it unbelievable that jurors in such a highly charged case could be shown such a potentially prejudicial film at any point during the trial, much less with their deliberations in sight. They immediately moved for a mistrial, which was denied, even though one of the last images provided by the court for the panel was the truncated King clip with its obviously troubling images of a police brutality case.

The trial judge also failed to instruct the jurors that it was the state's burden to prove that Nevers and Budzyn were not acting in self-defense, rather than the defense's responsibility to prove they were—a potentially fertile area of reasonable doubt.

During closing arguments, prosecutor Doug Baker presented Nevers as a murderous Neanderthal, "his club covered with blood, flushed with victory." Nevers had recalled the moments after the fight quite differently: "I felt relief. Someone else would take this man into custody. The struggle was finally over."

On August 23, the mostly black juries returned their verdicts against Nevers and Budzyn: guilty of second-degree murder. Lessnau, who faced life in prison, was acquitted by the trial judge. When the verdicts were returned, Budzyn sat staring straight ahead. Nevers, his head in his hands, began sobbing.

"In a matter of five minutes, his entire career has gone down the tubes," said Nevers's lawyer, Goldpaugh. Judge Crockett allowed Nevers and Budzyn to remain free on bail pending their sentencing, but made it clear this was not motivated to allow them more time with their families and friends. "Their imprisonment at this point," Crockett said, "might prove to be dangerous to them without special arrangements."

Mayor Coleman Young announced that justice had been done. The defense attorneys announced they would appeal.

The sentencings of the two cops were set for October 18. A badly shaken Nevers told the Detroit News that he was stunned by the verdicts.

"I couldn't believe it," the veteran cop said. "I honestly, in my heart, thought this jury would put aside all the pressures they were under and listen to the facts. But obviously, they didn't."

Budzyn said nothing, but Nevers's comments turned out to be right on the money when it came to his partner's case. The lone white juror on that panel called a Detroit radio show the day after the verdict to speak with Budzyn's attorney, Michael Batchelor. The attorney, who is black, had endured months of threats and insults for his work representing the accused officer. What he heard next was perhaps the lowest point yet for the defense lawyer.

"I really feel I owe [Budzyn] an apology," said the caller, who identified himself only as Karl. During the eight days of deliberations, Karl had argued for an involuntary manslaughter conviction, which carried a much-reduced jail term. But the pressure of being the lone white juror became too much, and he finally caved in to the majority's point of view.

Batchelor buried his head in his hands at the revelation. The juror later spoke with the Associated Press and provided more details.

"I had a bad feeling about my decision all along," he said. "But I did it. I can't change it. That's where the apology came in." The juror also said that in violation of the judge's orders, jurors on the case were watching television reports and reading newspaper articles about the case. This allowed them to learn that Nevers was a member of a 1970s police unit called STRESS (Stop The Robberies, Enjoy Safe Streets). The unit, which was never brought up during the trial since it could prove prejudicial to the officer, had a horrible reputation in the African-American community.

It also allowed jurors to hear that the National Guard had been activated and certain roads shut down in anticipation of possible riots if Nevers and Budzyn were acquitted.

The stunning apology did little to boost Budzyn's spirits, but the news about the jurors ignoring the judge's admonition regarding news reports would turn out to be quite important down the road.

Neither Budzyn nor Nevers got life, but both received stiff sentences from Crockett at a highly charged sentencing hearing. The two cops spoke, as did Green's estranged wife, Rose Mary Green, who came up from North Carolina.

"It is time for the world to see through the excuses and face the truth—being black, unemployed, and having used drugs did not kill Malice," she said, putting the lie to claims that race was responsible for the fatal encounter and putting it on the two veteran cops. "Mr. Budzyn and Mr. Nevers killed my husband."

Budzyn, in tears, apologized for Green's death but reasserted his innocence. "I was just doing my job," he said, his stoic demeanor disappearing in the face of jail time, his voice barely audible. "I never struck Mr. Green—never."

Crockett then delivered his sentences: twelve to twenty-five years for Nevers, eight to eighteen years for Budzyn. In a bizarre tribute to their law enforcement prowess, both men were assigned to the federal prison system rather than the Michigan state system.

"In the state system, it's entirely possible that former police officers could come in contact with people they've put behind bars," said a corrections department spokesman. Yet not even a move to the federal system in Michigan was eventually enough protection; the pair was shifted to the Fort Worth (Texas) Federal Correctional Institution in mid-November.

It may have made them safer, but it also made them lone-
lier. Family members and friends were now faced with a long
trip to see the jailed officers. Budzyn's daughter, Andrea, and
his grandsons—both born after he went to jail—could not
afford the plane tickets to see him. He met his first grandson,
Zachary, in a one-shot prison visit. The second, Alec, existed
only in the photos hanging inside Budzyn's prison locker.

The case no longer made headlines, but it didn't go away.
In May 1994, Crockett—while saying their arguments on
appeal had some merit—turned down a defense request for
new trials. The appeals process dragged on. And on. And on.

Lessnau fared better in his next court appearance. In
January 1995, the Detroit Law Department found that he
was entitled to $437,500 to settle a lawsuit asserting he was
unfairly treated in the aftermath of the Green case. He
remains a patrol cop in Detroit's Seventh Precinct.

Lessnau was not the only officer among the seven at 23rd
and Warren to benefit eventually from the city's mishandling
of the incident. Lessnau's partner, Officer Karl Gunther, settled with the city in 1997 for $1.02 million, as did Officer Paul
Goteleaere and Officer James Kijek. Sgt. Freddie Douglas,
who is still appealing his conviction on a misdemeanor charge
in the case, received a $350,000 settlement from the city for
denial of due process.

Kijek turned into an emotional wreck after facing the
ultra-public allegations and his subsequent suspension. He
suffered from insomnia and crying spells, and dropped
twenty pounds in a matter of weeks. He was reinstated to the
department after six months, but could not readjust to street

work and took early retirement one week later. He has never held another job.

Nevers and Budzyn continued doing their time in Texas. The first anniversary of their incarceration arrived on October 12, 1994. Five months later, the Michigan Court of Appeals upheld their convictions. Generating money to keep the legal process rolling was no easy task as the lawyers' costs soared and the months rolled by.

Anniversary No. 2 came up and still no appeal.

Anniversary No. 3 rolled by one year later. During this year in prison, Budzyn missed his father's funeral.

Three months before the two cops would mark their fourth year behind bars, there was finally a breakthrough for Budzyn. On July 31, 1997, the Michigan Supreme Court—the state's highest court—reversed his conviction and proclaimed Walter Budzyn a free man.

The court cited the screening of Malcolm X for the jurors, noting that its monologue attacking the white race "might have triggered an emotional response from the jury, because defendants' conduct, as alleged, could arguably fit the description given by Malcolm X's character." The film's "forceful words and images" could have undermined the jury's ability to reach an impartial verdict in the case, the court decided.

The panel ruled there was more when reversing Budzyn's second-degree murder conviction. The city officials' decision to suspend the officers before the trial could have been prejudicial to the defendants, the judges said. As was the city's multimillion dollar settlement with the Green family before any of the officers was found criminally liable for the incident, they added.

There was one bit of sad business to tend to before Budzyn's return home: bidding farewell to his prison roommate, Nevers. Budzyn's final promise to Nevers, as he left their mutual cell: "I'm going to keep up the fight." The pair had received news of the court's decision at the last minute, and had just fifteen minutes together before Budzyn's departure. A friend later recalled that Nevers was "devastated, absolutely devastated" when Budzyn left.

Nevers, in a call to a Detroit radio station, told its listeners, "I wish to God I could go with him, but I can't."

Budzyn was released and reunited with his family, a day that he thought might not ever come. The ex-cop put out a videotaped statement saying he was eager to see his wife, his daughter, his grandsons. He held eight-month-old Alec for the first time, and went to his visit his father's grave. Supporters planning a welcome home bash had trouble finding a big enough venue to hold the crowd.

"I also want to thank the Michigan Supreme Court," Budzyn said on his video, "for finally doing justice in my case."

The state court's decision had one unlikely supporter: Green's father, Jessie. "Everybody deserves a second chance," he told a Detroit television station.

The same Michigan judges, despite the same legal arguments, rejected Nevers' appeal for a new trial. The case against Budzyn was not as clear-cut, the judges decided, since Nevers had acknowledged—and the city medic had agreed—that he struck Green in the head with his flashlight. Nevers' wife, Nancy, held a news conference suggesting her husband had become a political prisoner of sorts.

"The NAACP, Coleman Young, and a radical fringe in the city of Detroit have all won today," she announced. "They have succeeded in holding us hostage.... This denial for a fair trial for Larry Nevers is an obscene miscarriage of justice."

Budzyn arrived in Detroit a day later. Asked if he had a hard time saying goodbye to Nevers at the Texas penitentiary, he replied with a simple, "Yes."

With the now fifty-one-year-old Budzyn out, prosecutors had a decision to make: should they retry the officer who had already spent three-plus years behind bars? Two weeks after Budzyn returned home, he had an answer: Yes. Prosecutors ran down eight witnesses from the first trial and decided to do the whole thing one more time. Transcripts of the old case were dredged up, memories were jogged, old notes reviewed.

But things had changed. The emotionally charged atmosphere, the racially charged attitudes, were gone. Late in 1997, Coleman Young died. Walter Budzyn was back in Michigan with his family. Yet it was still hanging over his head. Nearly six years after their first and only encounter, Walter Budzyn could not escape Malice Green.

For a while, it seemed that was true for Nevers, too— only worse. Budzyn would have another shot at redemption, at vindication. But the fifty-seven-year-old Nevers was still taking three meals a day in a prison-issue jumpsuit in Texas. That situation changed, improbably, on New Year's Eve.

On that day, Nevers walked out of prison, a free man for the first time in more than four years. A federal judge had ruled one day earlier that his second-degree murder conviction should also be overturned. Nevers caught a taxicab to the Dallas-Fort Worth Airport and flew off for an emotional reunion with his wife.

U.S. District Court Judge Lawrence Zatkoff went even further than the judges who freed Budzyn. The trial should have been moved from Detroit, he ruled, because of the massive pretrial publicity. Their access to local news reports allowed jurors to hear that people were predicting a Los Angeles-type riot if the jurors acquitted the two officers, Zatkoff said. That same access allowed jurors to hear that Nevers was a member of the controversial STRESS unit.

"The guilt or innocence of petitioner Larry Nevers... is not at issue in this case," Zatkoff wrote in his eighty-eight-page decision. "What is at issue is the question of whether [Nevers] was afforded his constitutional right to a fair trial. To allow [his] criminal conviction to stand, under the circumstances presented here, would run counter to the constitutional guarantees of the Sixth Amendment."

The proud Nevers had refused to allow his family to see him as an inmate, preferring to leave them with the vision of him as a police officer rather than a prisoner. When he heard the news in prison that he would finally see his wife after four years, he wept.

"He said," Nancy Nevers related, "'I'm going to see your face.'"

Nevers's appeals attorney, Neil Fink, said his client would be happy to testify on Budzyn's behalf at his retrial.

Prosecutors, for their part, said they planned to appeal Zatkoff's ruling; even if they're not successful, Nevers will likely face a second trial at some point.

"He wants to clear his name," said Nancy Nevers. "And the only way to do that is another trial."

Budzyn wants to do the same. Just weeks before the start of his retrial, he held a news conference to make his first public statement since his release. It was short and to the point.

"I know that some people have reacted to me not speaking publicly before now, but I believe my case should be decided in a courtroom," he said. "I gave nineteen-and-a-half years of my life protecting the people of this community. I've protected you, and I've protected your families. All I ask now is that if you're called upon to decide this case that you be fair and have an open mind.

"I did not kill Malice Green. I've waited four years for this trial. I look forward to proving my innocence."

The jury that heard this case, unlike the previous one, was racially diverse—eight whites, three blacks and an Asian. A change in the local court structure ensured a jury pool that was 57 percent white, 40 percent black. One of the new jurors was an ex-cop's wife; her husband had worked in the same precinct as Budzyn.

"I feel like his time was served," she said during pre-trial questioning by the attorneys. "He didn't do the actual beating."

Budzyn was cautiously optimistic as he returned to court for his second go-round.

Things had changed since the first trial; for one thing, the case was dubbed "The Police Murder Trial" and carried live to a national audience on Court TV. The jury pool was obviously altered. And the heightened racial atmosphere that surrounded the first case had dissipated over the last 4 1/2 years. *60 Minutes* had done a piece on the Malice Green case that was favorable to the officers involved. There was reason for Budzyn to be optimistic.

A mostly white jury was selected for Michigan vs. Budzyn II: eight whites, three blacks, one Asian. It was in many ways a repeat of the first trial, right down to Budzyn's emotional recounting of the night that Malice Green died.

Defense attorney Carole Stanyar said Budzyn was simply a cop doing his job when they tried to arrest Green. He "heard nothing indicating a man was being beaten to death," she said. Stanyar stressed that Budzyn had never struck Green with his flashlight. The cocaine in Green's system was raised as something that could have made him overly aggressive or contributed to his death.

There was one weird twist in the trial, something entirely new: Budzyn turned in a man who was willing to provide him with perjured testimony to aid his case. The man told Budzyn that he would testify that he had seen everything on that November night; he asked the officer for information and photographs to prepare his bogus testimony.

Budzyn turned him in. Once a cop, always a cop.

Budzyn took the stand to again say that he had never struck Green. Prosecutors mounted an intense cross-examination, but Budzyn remained resolute in his version of the events. He answered questions in the same low, monotonous voice that marked his 1993 testimony. The trial lasted just twelve days.

When the jury returned its verdict on March 19, after six days of deliberations, it was a split decision: No murder conviction, but guilty of involuntary manslaughter. Given his time already spent behind bars, Budzyn faced a likely sentence of time served at his April 17 sentencing.

That was not enough for one of Budzyn's lawyers, James Howarth. "It's like being kicked in the stomach," he said, promising an appeal. "I know Walter... and we're going to the Court of Appeals. He doesn't like this little crumb."

Members of both the Green and Budzyn families sobbed in the courtroom. Budzyn said absolutely nothing. Nevers, who watched the verdict on television at a friend's house, did the same, but his attorney expressed confidence that his client would fare better in his second go-round with a jury. The cocaine in Green's system was as much to blame as anything that Larry Nevers did, the lawyer said.

"It'd be like grabbing a hemophiliac by the arm and then he bleeds to death," said attorney Neil Fink. "Grabbing his arm would not normally be unreasonable force."

While the previous murder convictions had been greeted with delight by Green's backers and relief from many others in Detroit, Budzyn's second conviction found people wondering if he was the victim.

"How many times can you kill a man?" asked Detroit News columnist Pete Waldmeir. "Not Malice Green—I'm talking about Walter Budzyn. His life was ruined once. Now, though he'll probably never serve another day in jail, he's been ruined again." According to Waldmeir, Budzyn was guilty of one thing: "Doing his job."

If there is a fitting epitaph for this long, involved, political, racially divisive case—if there could be a fitting epitaph—it might have come from Detroit police union head Tom Schneider. On the day of the verdicts against Budzyn and Nevers, he spoke a simple truth that no one had broached in all the rhetoric and all the vitriol that came with the case.

"These situations," he said, "simply will not occur if the person about to be arrested simply complies with the orders of the officers involved."

*Chapter 4*

# ROBERT LEAKS

## *THE STRAWBERRY INCIDENT*

**ACCORDING TO *MONEY* MAGAZINE,** it is the most dangerous city in the United States: Newark, northern New Jersey's
most populous city, a fifteen-minute train ride from
Manhattan. Some of New York's most famous citizens—
Mayor Edward I. Koch, singer-songwriter Paul Simon—were
born in the city across the Hudson in Newark.

For ten years, Officer Robert Leaks had patrolled
Newark's gritty streets without incident, compiling a solid if
not sensational record. That changed forever in a few short
minutes on a warm Saturday evening on a Newark street corner. There, Officer Leaks—a cop with a reputation for
aggressively targeting the street-level drug dealers who had
choked Newark for the past thirty years—observed what
appeared to be a typical corner drug deal.

The alleged buyer was known for blocks around as
"Strawberry." Dannette Daniels was her given name, but her
rap sheet portrayed something far different from her sweet,

agrarian sobriquet. She had a criminal record going back more than a decade, mostly for possession and sale of drugs. That night, the night her actions forever changed two lives— hers and the officer's—Daniels was wanted on an outstanding warrant after ignoring a scheduled court appearance in central New Jersey.

As Leaks moved in to make his arrest, Daniels began screaming and shouting that the police were hassling a pregnant woman.

**Why? Why was the police shooting of an inebriated, gun-toting man characterized as a racial shooting? The officer was white. The victim was black.**

A crowd sympathetic to the woman's claims quickly assembled, making Leaks's already difficult task— arresting a screaming drug suspect on a busy intersection—even more dicey. As the angry crowd swelled, Leaks tried to handle his task as quickly as possible. The encounter instead ended with Dannette Daniels, who tried to hijack Leaks's police car, dead from a single gunshot fired by the officer.

Leaks, feeling lucky to be alive, thought that would be the end of it. But the shooting didn't finish anything; it just started it all. By the time it was over, Officer Leaks would watch his reputation being dragged through the mud and his mayor temporarily take away his livelihood, and wait for the day when he would be vindicated.

A group of local demonstrators, the Zoo Crew, helped organize protests against Leaks; five of its members testified against him as "eyewitnesses." The group that slandered Leaks's good name was later exposed as a wholesaler of heroin and cocaine—in fact, Newark's biggest. Because Leaks was black, there was no cry of racism from the protesters; instead, they spread insidious lies portraying the cop, who was only doing his job, as a cold-blooded killer who fatally shot Daniels because she had spurned his sexual advances.

The shooting was the nineteenth involving Newark police officers in 1997, and the third fatal incident. None of the others included such a volatile mix of rumor and innuendo.

"Not in my twenty years on the job have I ever seen anything like this," said Jack McEntee, head of the Newark police union. "These incidents always stir up someone, but this was a unique case. What made it unique was the people who were saying these things and their credibility. That's what bothered us the most."

It would take three months before Leaks was vindicated, ninety-two agonizing days during which he didn't collect a paycheck and wondered whether he would ever get his job back. And even after finally being cleared, he took one more financial kick from the city officials who had so quickly hung him out to dry.

Newark is the stereotypical crumbling metropolis, a once-proud city still struggling to right itself thirty years after the riots that almost destroyed it and turned the city into a national symbol of urban blight.

Three centuries earlier, in May 1666, thirty families came down by boat from Connecticut and settled the land in what would become the city of Newark.

By the 1930s Newark had become almost a sister city to the neighboring Big Apple. The New York Yankees' top farm team, the Newark Bears, were the talk of the town, and future Yankee greats like Red Rolfe, Joe Gordon, and Spud Chandler entertained the locals. But there were already signs of the great collapse to come; suburban flight was undermining the city even before World War II.

**The mythology—half-truths, oft-repeated rumors, downright inaccuracies—seemed to have a life of its own, but little to do with what actually happened.**

By 1939 Newark was home to just 11 percent of the state's jobs; thirty years earlier, that figure had been 20 percent. And 31 percent of its housing units were deemed below standards "of health and decency," a city-financed planning report found.

But the city fought gamely until the 1960s, when the arrest of a black cab driver on July 12, 1967, ignited the tinderbox of emotions in the city's Central Ward, a nest of political corruption. The unprecedented Newark riots brought the city to its knees.

By the time it was over, five days later, the total of the destruction was staggering: 26 dead, more than 1,500 wounded, more than 1,600 arrested, and more than $10 million in property damage, which included the devastation of more than 1,000 stores.

"It is all gone," said Mayor Hugh Addonizio, whose conviction on federal corruption charges followed three years later. "The whole town is gone. It is all over."

Newark became the butt of jokes and one of the nation's most dangerous places to live—for those who dared to stay in the city. The population dropped—it currently stands at 275,000—and the number of criminals soared. Street-corner drug operations flourished, and crack became king in many neighborhoods. Relations between the local community and the local police were never fully repaired; few in Newark were shocked when the latest police director, William Celester, was jailed himself on fraud and corruption charges.

Robert Leaks knew little of this history when he arrived on the job in Newark in 1987, a twenty-three-year-old transplant from the South.

Leaks had come north from South Carolina to live with a relative in Newark, arriving in 1982 to run his uncle's combination barber shop and candy store in the city's South Ward. He adapted quickly to his new locale and decided to stay. He joined the Newark police department in 1987.

Leaks met his wife Reba in Newark and started a family there; the couple had two sons.

The cop made a good name for himself in the department, earning praise and commendations from his superiors. He became known for his relentless pursuit of the Newark drug trade during six years as a beat cop in the city's West District. After three years in the sex crimes unit, he switched over to the South Precinct on Labor Day 1996, part of a new "quality of life" patrol meant to cut back street crime in the bad neighborhood.

Popular with his fellow cops, Detective Leaks was known to all simply as Bobby. Fellow cops recalled him as a straight arrow who often spoke of his wife and kids, a real stand-up guy.

"A gentleman, a good person," said McEntee, head of the city's Fraternal Order of Police. "We were proud to have him as a member. His reputation was beyond reproach."

Fellow detective Derrick Hatcher echoed McEntee, describing Leaks as an "exemplary officer." Even his critics— and there would soon be plenty of those—never said Leaks was a bad cop, a brutal cop, a crooked cop. Nobody ever said that about Bobby Leaks.

On the night of June 7, 1997, Leaks was driving in an unmarked police car with his partner, Officer Michael Johnson. They cruised through a neighborhood known for heavy drug trafficking, eyes peeled for the telltale signs of dope dealers and dope fiends.

It didn't take long to find some.

As they approached the corner of Clinton Avenue and Chadwick Street, they spotted Dannette Daniels involved in an apparent drug deal with a thirteen-year-old boy. Daniels's four-year-old son, Marlon, stood nearby watching his mother trying to score some crack.

Daniels was known to street cops as a drug user, and her prior record included at least eight arrests.

Daniels had received a three-year jail term in 1991 after a drug sale conviction, and she was arrested for crack possession in 1987, 1988, and 1995. Three months before this balmy June night, she had been arrested for dealing cocaine within a thousand feet of a local grammar school. And she was wanted by police in Woodbridge, New Jersey, after she failed to appear there on charges of receiving stolen property.

She used a variety of aliases to keep herself on the street, authorities said.

The thirteen-year-old boy bolted once the cops arrived, and Johnson took off after the youth. Leaks arrested Daniels at the scene and loaded her into the back seat of the police car; since it was an unmarked car, there was no cage separating the front and rear seats, a factor that turned out to be vital. A crowd had started to gather as Leaks did his job, and the people began to grow angry. Daniels was shouting, decrying the officer's efforts and inciting the crowd.

Leaks had trouble keeping handcuffs on Daniels's thin wrists. Daniels, the handcuffs dangling from one wrist, continued to struggle with Leaks, and eventually wormed her way into the driver's seat of the car. The keys were in the ignition. The suspect quickly started the car and threw it into reverse. Leaks, who was trying to enter the car through the front passenger door, was struck by the swinging door as the car took off, and hung on for dear life as it accelerated.

As the car sped backwards, dragging Leaks along, the officer managed to pull his 9mm service revolver. He ordered her to stop the car; she refused and continued flying in reverse. Afraid for his life, Leaks fired one shot into the woman's neck. Mortally wounded, she crashed the car into a parked Nissan Maxima further down Clinton Avenue.

The parked car was catapulted ten feet onto the sidewalk by the speed of the police vehicle. Leaks was thrown into the car, where he was trapped in the wreckage with the body of the bleeding woman. The officer, who suffered lacerations on his face, hands, and wrists, and bruises on his right thigh and knee in the incident, was finally cut free of the twisted metal and taken to a nearby hospital for treatment.

Dannette "Strawberry" Daniels—a vial of cocaine in her possession—was pronounced dead at the scene at 9:35 PM, just twenty minutes after Leaks and his partner had spotted her. The mother of three was thirty-one.

The crowd on the street swelled, growing more and more hostile. When Leaks's attorney, Vincent Scocca, arrived on the scene, there were more than fifty police officers and two hundred people from the neighborhood milling about. Before the night was over, the tires were slashed on thirty police vehicles. Onlookers began hurling rocks and bottles at police. "It was almost like a staged event," Scocca recalled. "It was like something from a movie."

This "film" had a nasty plot twist; some people in the crowd started spreading vicious lies about Detective Robert Leaks.

Scocca remembers hearing the details of the carjacking and shooting, talking to others at the scene, and thinking that Leaks had acted properly. The head of the police union remembers that the preliminary call made at the scene was that the Leaks shooting was justifiable.

"The main question in any of these shootings, the bottom line, is to see if the use of force was justified," Scocca says. "In a situation like this, with eyewitness accounts that the officer was hanging from the car as it accelerated at a high rate of speed, it seemed clear that his life was in jeopardy and the use of force was justified.

"I thought at that point that the shooting was OK. This was not a situation where it wasn't justified force."

But some in the crowd began saying the shooting was unnecessary, that the officer didn't have to shoot the woman, that it could have been handled differently. The instigators, Scocca later recalled, included a number of people known to the police as drug dealers—members of an alleged drug-dealing gang called the Zoo Crew.

Some eyewitnesses related that Daniels was only borrowing a quarter from the teen on the corner, and that Leaks had beaten her before she stole the car. Stories varied wildly from eyewitness to eyewitness, raising immediate questions about credibility.

"It was very clear early on that some of the people pointing fingers had previous involvement with law enforcement," Scocca said. "The police had [previously] arrested some of these people."

What Scocca didn't know, and what the Zoo Crew didn't know, was that the U.S. attorney's office was, on this very night, getting close to wrapping up a widespread probe of the Crew's activities. The probe had started more than a year earlier. Once the involvement of the Zoo Crew in the Daniels case became clear, the joint task force investigating the alleged drug operation dropped two Newark police officers from the team.

They didn't want any conflict-of-interest charges ruining their investigation, or clouding the probe of the Daniels's shooting.

Leaks, getting his wounds treated at Newark's University Hospital, was unaware of the ruckus back at the scene. He knew nothing about the other investigation. And he certainly couldn't have known what was about to come.

Investigations were immediately launched by the police department, the Essex County prosecutor's office, and the state attorney general's office. The mayor of Newark, Sharpe James, did not feel compelled to wait for their completion before rendering his decision on Leaks.

Two days after the shooting, the Zoo Crew mounted a protest march on City Hall. The self-proclaimed community activists invited marchers to gather outside their Newark sportswear store and march on the local police precinct. Terrence "Mustafa" Dent, the head of the crew, told the crowd that he hoped one day to slap handcuffs around Leaks's wrists personally.

Eventually, the crowd of 250 descended on City Hall. They wanted something done to Leaks, and they wanted it done immediately—due process be damned.

It was here that Daniels's sympathizers made their most outrageous allegation, and where Sharpe James decided to take their word over that of a decorated, ten-year veteran cop who had nearly given his life for the city of Newark.

James Williams VII, the slain woman's older brother, charged that Leaks had tried to romance the victim and that the officer had known the woman's family since he was a child. It was not true; Leaks grew up in South Carolina and was happily married. He and his wife had recently moved to a $212,000 dream home in South Jersey, a place to raise their young family. But that didn't stop the allegations from spreading.

"He tried to date her, and she refused," Williams insisted. "I've known him since he was a young boy. He knew her personally."

The mayor met with some of the family members—a courtesy he did not extend to Leaks—and emerged to address the protesters. "I have taken steps to immediately suspend the police officer without pay until a thorough investigation has been completed," James said. "There is an allegation by the family that the officer knew the woman, even dated her, and these are allegations that warrant an investigation."

There were already two investigations under way, both of which James ignored in playing to the crowd. And though the allegation was easy to check out—most folks on the force knew that Leaks had grown up closer to Newark, Delaware, than Newark, New Jersey—James never bothered to corroborate Williams' charges.

He simply suspended Leaks.

Newark political activist Ras Baraka, the son of poet Amiri Baraka, told the crowd flatly, "Robert Leaks is a murderer. He killed two people: Strawberry and her child."

As it turned out, Strawberry was not pregnant. But that rumor, and the lies about her relationship with Leaks, lingered throughout the case. The stories were printed and repeated, until they became almost part of the case, true or not. And of course James's decision went a long way to giving the charges credibility, Leaks's fellow officers believed.

Scocca said comments by the Zoo Crew that denigrated the officer stemmed from their desire to get a tough, no-nonsense cop off the street. Leaks was making forty to fifty gun and drug arrests per month, and that was cutting into their illicit drug business.

Leaks was suddenly out of work, wondering where the next mortgage payment on that dream house would come from. James had made a point of suspending him without pay.

"Put yourself in his position," says McEntee, the police union head. "You've just done one of the most difficult things you could ever have to do—take someone's life in defense of your own. And now you've got to sit and have coffee with your wife and read all this stuff in the papers. All because you're trying to arrest a drug dealer."

What most infuriated McEntee was that James, apparently bowing to political pressure, had deviated from standard policy in a police-involved shooting. Ordinarily, the officer who pulls the trigger is placed on administrative duty pending the completion of an investigation.

"You don't take food away from his table," McEntee said in his plainspoken way, "before an investigation."

McEntee and Leaks's fellow police officers decided to do something for their suspended colleague. They began by collecting $2,474 during an impromptu support session for Leaks. Over time, it was donations from colleagues and his wife's steady paycheck that allowed the family to keep its home.

At the first City Council meeting after the shooting, dozens of residents lined up to decry police brutality. Feeling that Leaks was being left dangling during all this, the Fraternal Order of Police decided to take its own action.

On June 18 about five hundred off-duty Newark cops held their own march on City Hall—this time to let James know that they felt Bobby Leaks was getting screwed. Officers on horseback joined officers playing bagpipes during the march.

"Bring back Bobby!" they shouted. Several sported shirts that read "The Blue Crew," a jibe at the Zoo Crew. They made it clear that they felt the Zoo Crew bunch was using the shooting to incite anti-police sentiment. Detective Hatcher observed drily that some of Leaks's accusers "are not by any standards considered to be pillars of the community."

When James attempted to speak to the officers, they simply turned their backs on him. "Sharpe must go!" they shouted at the mayor.

James seemed shocked by the angry police reaction. "This tragedy has had too much name-calling, too many marches... too much political grandstanding," said James, who had done his own grandstanding at the previous march.

McEntee, to much applause, told the crowd, "We think Bobby Leaks was wronged. He was suspended without a hearing. We want a complete and thorough investigation."

The angry cops took a page out of the earlier protesters' book, amending their usual chant—"No justice! No peace!"—into something more cop-friendly. "No justice!" they thundered. "No police!"

People walking past the rally showed how quickly the rumors about Leaks's purported relationship with the victim had spread. "It was wrong. The woman was pregnant," Newark resident Keisha McNeil told the Newark Star-

Ledger. "He should be suspended. Actually, he should be fired."

But Councilwoman Mildred Crump was cheered after she ripped James's decision to suspend Leaks. "Drug dealers get due process," she observed. "Shouldn't we give police officers due process as well?"

It didn't matter. The rally ended. The mayor left. It was politics as usual. And Bobby Leaks was still suspended without pay.

The prosecutor's office continued its investigation of the case as Leaks sweated out its decision. His lawyer, Scocca, was afraid his client would be a sacrificial lamb, the victim of "a political lynching."

"The political aspects complicated the case," he says now. "If you try to look at it from a purely legal angle, you realize it's justified. But you throw the political angle into the equation, and it gets complicated. I was afraid it would be colored in that sense—there would be a motivation to indict Leaks to appease certain elements of the community."

Despite his fears, Leaks opted to testify before the grand jury. It was his call to make; he could choose not to cooperate and hope the facts would speak for themselves. But Leaks wanted the jury to hear directly from him what happened, to let them know what went on that night at the corner of Clinton and Chadwick.

It was, and remains, the only time that Leaks has ever spoken publicly about the case. He turned down a recent interview request, preferring, once again, to let the facts in the case speak for themselves. Scocca said his client wants his life to return to normal—a longshot hope, at best.

"My concern wasn't as to what Robert Leaks would say to the jury," Scocca said. "My concern was what the members of the community were going to say, what was their motivation for testifying. The truth is a constant. If you tell the truth—and Robert Leaks was telling the truth—that's a constant."

Although grand jury proceedings are secret, some word did leak out. And it seems that some of the eyewitness accounts lacked the ring of authenticity that characterized Leaks's tale. While the scientific evidence seemed to match up with Leaks's story, there were discrepancies between the forensics and the stories some witnesses told. Five members of the Zoo Crew were reportedly among those who testified.

The twenty-three–member grand jury heard from Leaks and another fifty-six witnesses over six weeks that summer; only twelve of them, a simple majority, had to vote yes to return an indictment against Leaks. When Essex County Prosecutor Clifford J. Minor announced its findings on September 4, he attempted to put the case's many lies to rest.

No, he said, Dannette Daniels was not pregnant. No, he continued, there was no evidence that she and Leaks had been dating. No, the autopsy did not indicate that Daniels had been beaten. And no, Officer Robert Leaks would not be charged with any crime in the shooting.

"By declining to indict the officer on any criminal charge, it can be concluded that the jury felt the force used by Officer Leaks was justified under all of the circumstances," Minor said.

Undaunted by Strawberry's role in her own death, the Daniels family said it planned to sue the city of Newark over the shooting and filed the necessary legal paperwork. There was also discussion of a federal civil rights probe of the shooting—an enterprise that would determine if a black police officer shot a black drug buyer because of her race.

A Daniels family adviser, the Rev. William Simmons, acknowledged that Leaks was not responsible for the lifestyle that landed Dannette Daniels on the corner of Clinton Street that night. "There are a lot of Strawberries up and down our community reaching out for help," Simmons said. "The conditions that bred these Strawberries should not be allowed to exist."

And family friend Shahid Watson actually praised the work of the grand jury: "Investigators have been fair. Nothing has been swept under the rug." But even this was not enough to appease some who would never be swayed on the topic of Leaks's guilt.

"These are all lies," said poet/activist Amiri Baraka. "They knew from the beginning that they weren't going to indict this man. The justice system is a charade. We should call Ray Charles and Stevie Wonder to see if they can see through this." For some, rhetoric would never give way to reality.

Paul Mulshine, columnist for the Newark Star-Ledger, felt differently.

"Leaks went from being a cop who had made a split-second decision in a tough situation to being a cop accused of committing murder in a cheap attempt to get romance from a pregnant druggie," he wrote once the dust had cleared. "This is a tough rap against any man, but particularly rough for one who has a wife and two kids."

Leaks, upon hearing of the grand jury's decision "felt a tremendous sense of relief," Scocca said. The cleared cop said nothing publicly, but was anxious to get back on the job.

On August 28, the day after the grand jury completed its investigation of the Leaks shooting incident, a federal task force moved throughout Essex County making arrests—twenty-three in all before the sun came up that morning. The suspects seized in the early morning series of raids were allegedly involved in a lucrative drug ring operating in Newark. And all of its members, federal authorities said, belonged to the Zoo Crew.

Authorities seized thousands of vials filled with crack cocaine—so many that they were initially unable to count them.

According to a federal prosecutor, the Zoo Crew had used its four legitimate businesses—a sporting goods store, a flower shop, a fast food joint, and an auto parts store—as fronts to move drugs from New York into Newark. They dealt four hundred pounds of cocaine and heroin annually, generating an estimated $10 million a year in revenue.

The investigation showed the crew also harbored an obsessive hatred for the police. According to the indictment, crew members threatened to "blow the heads off" any undercover officers who attempted to infiltrate their operation.

U.S. Attorney Faith Hochberg was unimpressed by the gang's community efforts, which included running a local basketball league and marching on City Hall to protest police brutality. "You can dress it up, you can sponsor a basketball team, you can open a flower shop, but you're still a drug dealer," she told a news conference. "Behind that nice façade was a very sophisticated and lucrative drug-dealing opera-tion."

The group's public persona was simply a cover for its real business. Authorities said the people who actually lived in the neighborhoods with the Zoo Crew were wise to them; it was their complaints that prompted the investigation.

Ironically, some of these same people booed passing Newark police cars for days following the Daniels shooting.

The raid was not a total success. Terrence Dent, the Zoo Crew's reputed kingpin, had managed to elude the wide net thrown out by federal authorities—perhaps in one of the two $90,000 Mercedes-Benzes that he paid cash to lease, all of it in $10 and $20 bills. The man who had hoped to put hand-cuffs on Leaks was now a fugitive on the run.

"If you shine a light on people, sooner or later you'll show them for what they are," McEntee said. "Dent's somewhere out there, hiding under a rock. Sooner or later, he'll run out of money or they'll put him on *America's Most Wanted*. "He's got his day coming."

Leaks was finally restored to active duty on September 11, more than three months after the night that he must live with forever. But despite his previous outstanding field work, authorities opted not to put Leaks back in his old job. Instead, he was placed at a desk job—a newly minted paper jockey.

"What we've done is temporarily placed him in an admin-istrative assignment... until we can make some determina-tion where he's going to be working in the future," said police director Joseph Santiago, the replacement for the corrupt

Celester. "I don't think it would serve any purpose to put him back in the situation he faced."

Once his suspension was lifted, Leaks was entitled to the back pay denied him during the time that he was kept off the job. Collecting ninety-two days worth of pay at once was reason for Leaks to cheer up. Mayor James, after all, had promised as much in a television interview: "If the officer is found innocent of all charges, he will not lose any pay whatsoever. He will be fully reimbursed."

It didn't turn out that way.

A departmental hearing found that Leaks had made some errors in his handling of the Daniels case, specifically his failure to handcuff the suspect. He was also criticized for leaving the keys in the unmarked car's ignition. And he failed to call dispatchers when the crowd watching the arrests began to swell and grow unruly.

The findings were legitimate. According to the police union, the departmental panel ordered Leaks docked thirteen days' pay. Santiago, however, overruled the panel and raised the total to ninety-two days docked—the exact amount of time that Leaks had been on suspension.

"What a coincidence," sniffed union boss McEntee.

The police union did not forget. When the 1998 election season rolled around, they snubbed James. The union instead opted to endorse Councilwoman Crump, who had sprung to Leaks's defense. The politics of policing continue.

Leaks never received an apology from the mayor, not so much as a single phone call. Despite the grand jury findings and the prosecutor's clear statement exonerating the cop,

James went so far as to defend his decision to suspend the officer in the middle of the City Hall protest.

"The matter was handled correctly," the mayor insisted. "It was a tragic event in an emotionally charged environment that required a municipal response."

He still hasn't spoken to Bobby Leaks, who is back to carrying a gun and protecting the citizens of James's city.

## Chapter 5

# RAMIRO PENA

## *THE PICTURE'S WORTH A THOUSAND WORDS*

**THE FIRING OF RAMIRO PENA** was not national news.

The three-year police veteran had labored in obscurity in the Michigan town of Muskegon, working the midnight-to-8 AM shift. While most of the town's 38,809 residents were out and about, he was asleep. And when they were asleep, Ramiro Pena was responsible for protecting them. He was twenty-six years old, and he was good at his job.

At least he was until June 18, 1997, when Ramiro Pena was fired by the town fathers in the aftermath of a potentially deadly run-in between several police officers and a driver who might have killed them. Only their own efforts saved the cops' lives; Pena and the other officers, after a violent struggle, managed to arrest the driver, who was on probation for a pair of felony convictions and was drinking on the night of the incident.

Unlike other cases of alleged police brutality, such as those of Detroit officers Larry Nevers and Walter Budzyn, or the suburban Pittsburgh officers who arrested Jonny Gammage, there were no headlines from coast to coast, no visits from *60 Minutes,* no swarm of media around Ramiro Pena.

There was one link to those cases: Pena was offered up as a sacrifice to appease angry local groups who believed the beating was racially motivated. The Urban League of Muskegeon, the National Association for the Advancement of Colored People, and the Ad Hoc Committee for Equality and Justice were among the groups calling for somebody's head—anybody's head—in the case.

**Just 86 minutes after he answered the call to provide backup on a traffic stop, he became a murder suspect.**

Why? The driver of the car was black. Most of the arresting officers were white—although that didn't include Pena, who was of Mexican-American descent.

"I think they had to get somebody, you know what I mean?" said Fred LeMaire, the labor representative of Michigan's statewide Police Officers Labor Council. "I don't know if Pena was the easiest to grab—maybe. I know they looked at several people at the scene before he was charged."

When Pena was fired the whole thing was covered in an eight-paragraph dispatch from the Associated Press. His dismissal from the Muskegon police occurred June 18; the story about it didn't run until six days later. Here's how the AP summed it up:

"A police officer charged with assaulting a motorist, leading to public complaints of excessive force against blacks, has been fired. Ramiro Pena II was fired June 18.

"According to city civil service records and city officials, Pena was fired for using 'excessive force' against a motorist during an April traffic stop by police and for later making 'false statements to a supervisor.'"

The whole story ran barely two hundred words. But the tale of Ramiro Pena and his foray into the other side of the criminal justice system is hardly so simple.

The officer argues that he was the scapegoat for doing nothing more than his job—the same claims made by the officers in those higher-profile cases, claims that have led to overturned convictions and acquittals for those officers. During his April 23, 1997, encounter with Scottie Lee Waller—a meeting that landed Pena with an aggravated assault charge and Waller with lawyers lining up to sue the Muskegon police—the officer did only what he had learned from instructors in the police academy.

> **"The community wants someone's head. They still do," McCarthy said. "And the decision was made that someone will be served up. That was Ramiro Pena. He is the sacrificial lamb in this case."**

It wasn't Officer Pena who first spotted Waller driving a car with a stolen license plate in the early morning hours of that day in late spring—that was Officer Chris Mandoka. He wasn't even the second officer on the scene—that was Officer Chad Fellows. What happened after that is contained in a series of interviews conducted by investigators. This is the story as told by the officers on the scene that night.

Mandoka spotted Waller's 1969 Buick stopped in a closed gas station near Third and Muskegon streets, and he called in its license plate. There was a hit; the plate belonged on another car. The Buick pulled out of the gas station, and Mandoka turned on the lights atop the patrol car to pull the Buick over.

The car didn't stop.

Mandoka flipped the patrol car's siren on. The Buick continued for several blocks before pulling into a parking lot. It was about 1 AM.

Mandoka asked Waller for his license and registration, but the driver refused and kept his hands in his lap. Waller also refused to get out of the car upon being asked, and when Mandoka tried to pull him out, the driver grabbed the steering wheel and hung on tightly. Two other passengers were inside the car, and it was impossible for the officer to know if any or all of them were armed. None had showed that their hands were empty.

At about the same time, Fellows pulled in to back Mandoka and went through the same drill. Fellows ordered Waller out of the car, but Waller ignored him, too. As Fellows moved to put a headhold on Waller, the suspect slipped his car into gear and slammed his foot on the gas.

Like a rocket, the car burst forward with Waller in the driver's seat and Fellows holding onto him for dear life. Pena saw Mandoka hanging from the car, too. They covered twenty feet in a matter of seconds. Speaking later to a police investigator, Fellows recalled the absolute terror of those seconds.

"I thought I was going to get run over or injured, killed," Fellows said. "[This was] a 3,000-pound car that was pulling me along—I could be easily sucked underneath the tires."

Mandoka managed to jump clear of the accelerating car, and headed back to his police cruiser, expecting a chase to follow. But Waller was finally yanked from the moving vehicle by Fellows, landing on his head with the officer on top. Without Waller punching the gas pedal, the car slowed. One of the passengers reached over and turned off the key. With the car now stopped, Mandoka ran toward the vehicle—his gun in hand—approached Waller's car.

Pena, who had arrived shortly after Fellows, was stunned to see his fellow officers dangling from the side of the speeding vehicle. He ran back to his own cruiser to chase down the Buick. When the car stopped, he jumped from his vehicle and sprinted over to assist Fellows.

"Everything happened so fast," Pena recalled. "I heard the engine rev up, I saw them struggling. The vehicle took off, and I saw Officers Mandoka and Fellows still clinging to the car.... [It] took off fast."

Fellows, as he wrestled with Waller, was now screaming at the suspect: "Put your hands behind your back! Stop fighting! Stop resisting!" Pena, despite three years in the most dangerous shift in police work, had never seen anything like it. He remembered Waller as "agitated, angry, and combative... ignoring every lawful command... dangerous and extremely volatile."

Waller was at this point lying face down with his hands under his body. Pena could not see if Waller had a weapon of some sort beneath him, and so he tried to yank the suspect's hands into sight, scraping his knuckles on the parking lot asphalt. But Waller simply refused to cooperate with the officers' orders.

"Get your arms out!" Pena commanded vainly. "Get your arms out!"

The more they fought, the more irate Waller became. And the officers still didn't know if the suspect had a hidden gun or knife. Pena finally unleashed a blast of pepper gas into Waller's face, but with no discernable results.

In fact, the struggle grew worse.

A fourth officer on the scene, James Plouhar, recalled Pena "spraying [the pepper] directly right into his face." According to Plouhar, Waller simply became "more agitated." Pena then applied a series of pressure point holds on Waller: on the suspect's ear, near his chin, under his nose, exactly the way that Muskegeon's officers were taught to handle such incidents. When those proved equally fruitless, Pena landed several "brachial stuns" on the suspect—slamming a palm heel into the neck, one of the prescribed techniques to use during such incidents. Pena never denied landing those blows; he later told an investigator that he slammed Waller with "my whole force."

Meanwhile, Plouhar called the dispatcher for more cars. Waller was finally subdued and handcuffed. All the officers on the scene agreed that once Waller was in custody, once his wrists were secured, nobody landed any gratuitous blows on the suspect. On the contrary, Pena expressed concern about Waller's condition; the suspect was looking a little the worse for wear. Pena was a little beat up, too.

"I'm choking from the gas and I'm tired," he recalled later while testifying in response to a prosecutor's subpeona. "I'm exhausted."

Did he speak to Waller at all? "No," Pena said. Waller received two traffic tickets; a charge of resisting arrest was added later.

One of the passengers in the car told police that he was not surprised by Scottie Lee Waller's obstinacy in the face of such overwhelming authority. "Scottie's been that way," said Germaine Taylor, "ever since he was a kid."

As in the Rodney King case, there were two passengers in the car with Waller. And as in the King case, both passengers cooperated with police and were arrested without incident. Only the driver became combative; only the driver was involved in any altercation with the arresting officers.

There's no disputing that Waller looked awful when he arrived at the Hackley Hospital emergency room. His lower lip was grotesquely distended. Both his eyes were swollen shut. There was dried blood on the corner of his mouth, and scrapes on his forehead and the right side of his face. A Polaroid was taken of his battered face. And it was that picture which eventually became more important than the words of anybody who was at the scene of the fight.

Although Waller looked awful, his injuries were nowhere near as serious as they appeared. He had suffered no broken bones, no fractures of the face, nose, or jaw. Not a single one of his teeth was even loose. He did not require a single stitch. The medical term is "soft-tissue injuries"—injuries consistent with Pena's version of the attack, according to his lawyer.

Much of the swelling could have been a reaction to the pepper gas, which was sprayed directly into his face from point-blank range.

Waller made no claim of brutality to the emergency room staff. A nursing report described Waller as "alert and combative" upon arrival at the hospital. Mandoka had the same recollection; when an orderly offered Waller a chance to clean the pepper spray off his face, the suspect refused.

"(They) offered him a shower and he wouldn't take it," Mandoka said. "He was uncooperative."

When Waller was asked what happened, he told a nurse that "he was sprayed in the face with pepper gas, then his face struck the concrete while wrestling with police."

That story was soon to change.

Several of the driver's relatives arrived at the hospital and went ballistic at the sight of Waller's face. They began shouting about police brutality. And, according to the ER nurse's report, they were "using profanity, being loud and threatening to string somebody up."

By the time Waller had selected a lawyer and filed his $5.25 million lawsuit against the city and the Muskegon police, this was his version of what happened that night:

Without "cause or justification," Pena and the others sprayed pepper gas into his face to prevent Waller from identifying any of his assailants. They used a flashlight beneath his chin to hold his head up, slapped handcuffs on him, and then smashed him with nightsticks and fists while he lay helpless. The officers—including the Mexican-American Pena—augmented the beating with racial slurs: "black ass," "nigger," "bitch."

The laughing and joking officers never read Waller his rights, the lawsuit said. And the beating went on for five minutes, Waller claimed.

Nightsticks and fists to the face for five minutes. No broken bones. No loosened teeth. No facial fractures.

What followed was weeks of racial discord in Muskegon. Dozens of local residents began flooding city commission meetings to criticize the police department. And city leaders were condemned by local black leaders for failure to oversee their police officers properly.

Leaders of black organizations—the Urban League of Greater Muskegon, the NAACP, the Ad Hoc Committee for Equality and Justice—called for a meeting with Police Chief Edward Griffin to discuss the case. Many demanded that the officers on the scene that night be immediately dismissed. There were marches and vigils, and protesters handed out leaflets. Some demanded that Griffin be fired, too. A coalition of minority groups suggested the police department's "blue wall of silence" was protecting the cops at the scene, and they announced the establishment of their own complaint process for handling police brutality cases.

Political pressure was building; racial tensions were growing.

One of Pena's supporters, in a memo written several months later, noted that "it became clear that the Muskegon Police Department would have to offer up somebody's head." And as the turmoil continued, it became clear that head was going to belong to Pena.

Pena was suspended without pay while an investigation was conducted. Testimony from the other officers on the scene was vague; none said he had seen Pena punching Waller, and all said they had not beaten the suspect. The other officers were placed on administrative duty during the probe, a subtle sway of pitting them against Pena. Still, their testimony was far from conclusive.

"I didn't see it," Officer Fellows told investigators. "But, um, [I heard what] sounded like a punch.... I don't know how many."

Officer Plouhar said since he was calling for more backup, Pena and Waller were only in his peripheral vision. While he saw Pena strike the suspect, he could not determine if Pena's hand was open or closed—a vital distinction, the actual line between a beating and the proper way of handling an unruly suspect.

On June 17, 1997, Pena was accused of aggravated assault—a misdemeanor that carried a jail term of up to one year. Prosecutors alleged that Pena, with a closed fist, had rained fifteen to twenty blows on Waller's head and face. One day later, Pena was fired for using "excessive force" in the traffic stop and for making "false statements to a supervisor" in the subsequent investigation.

But despite the outcry from minority groups and the tale told by Waller, "no witnesses indicated there were any racial statements," said Muskegon County prosecutor Tony Tague.

None of the other officers at the scene were accused of any crime. They all subsequently returned to duty.

"There was no crime here," said Pena's attorney, Thomas McCarthy. "What we have is a man, in the person of Scottie

Waller, who refuses to cooperate in any fashion with the lawful directives of multiple police officers, who chooses to use potentially lethal force. He chooses to fight, and he becomes the recipient of some use of force.

"His injuries are remarkable in appearance.... That plays to the worst fears we all have about misuse of power," McCarthy continued. "But if you examine what took place, what Officer Pena did was appropriate."

Pena's supporters were stunned by the decision to fire him. Has anybody considered whether his actions might have prevented the violence from escalating to something worse? Didn't Pena follow the prescribed techniques taught by law enforcement instructors? Two use-of-force experts were expected to say just that when Pena's trial began.

Union head LeMaire said the suspension was typical of the way police officers rarely receive the constitutional rights routinely accorded the people they arrest: the presumption of innocence, the right to a fair trial. By firing Pena, a clear message was sent: Muskegon's powers that be considered the cop guilty.

"When other people are charged criminally, it's a different situation," LeMaire said. "You're upholding the laws out there, and now they're saying you broke those laws, how can I have you out there?

"Some departments will put you on light duty, or put you on administrative leave with pay. But they do not like to pay you while you're sitting at home."

Pena was an unlikely candidate for a police brutality complaint. During his three years working the midnight tour, according to McCarthy, he had never been disciplined or reprimanded for wrongful use of force. The only black mark on the officer's record was a traffic accident: his patrol car, while traveling too fast, skidded on an icy patch and slid into a light pole.

"I'm very impressed with Officer Pena," said McCarthy, who met with the defendant only after the Waller incident. "I think he's an honest, hard-working young man who is the victim himself of a highly politicized situation in the city of Muskegon.

"I believe he did not commit a crime."

A Muskegon jury would decide if McCarthy was right. Specifically, they would determine if Pena had gone beyond reasonable police force, had tried to physically injure Waller or cause serious injury, disfigurement, or impairment of health.

Before Ramiro Pena had his day in court, Scottie Walker went on trial in February 1998 for resisting arrest. Waller had already pleaded guilty to driving without a license and using a license plate that wasn't his—the very reason that police had stopped his car in the first place.

Walker faced up to a year in jail on those charges, along with additional time for violating his parole on two previous felony convictions. Waller's record was not quite as clean as that of Pena.

The six-member jury deliberated only an hour before acquitting Waller of resisting arrest; they then refused to discuss their verdict with reporters. Despite the license plate, the jurors told court officials that they felt police had no legitimate reason for stopping Waller—an illogical finding at best.

The acquittal came one month before jury selection began in the Pena case. Before the trial started, the defense was struck a pair of crippling blows: Their change of venue request was rejected. And their experts on appropriate police use of force would not be allowed to testify.

"That was worrisome," defense attorney McCarthy said later. "We had the best witnesses in the land. One of them had written the programs taught to Pena. But the judge knocked them out."

Pena had other problems. The cost of mounting his defense was growing exponentially. He was out of work. His father, Reynaldo Pena, had to cash in his pension to pay his son's legal bills.

His father was extraordinarily blunt about the cause of his son's woes: the city fathers surrendered to "radicals in the black community.... The state of Michigan is using my son as a political scapegoat."

Oddly enough, Reynaldo Pena wasn't alone in his feelings. William C. Muhammad, a Muskegon resident and Nation of Islam minister, echoed those words.

"I consider Mr. Pena a victim, a sacrificial lamb," he told the Muskegon Chronicle. "Some way, he got chosen (to prosecute)."

On March 10, 1998, Muskegon District Judge Richard J. Pasarela began prescreening potential jurors to determine if the pre-trial publicity had in any way prejudiced them against Pena. Pasarela met individually with each jury candidate to ensure that they had not formed any opinion of the case based on news reports.

It was the first time in Muskegon County history that a judge had gone to such pains to ensure an impartial jury. It turned out to be a bit of good news for Ramiro Pena.

A newspaper report said that Pena—facing a year in prison—"appeared relaxed and confident" as the trial began on March 16. Prosecutor Joseph Bader's opening argument was somewhat predictable: a police "code of silence" was protecting Pena. The officers destroyed evidence, and checked their reports against one another's to make sure everything fit.

In short, Pena and the other officers—none of them accused of any crime in connection with the case—had engaged in a conspiracy that night.

Ridiculous, McCarthy responded. Waller knew he was headed back to jail for a probation violation on the night that he was stopped. He had nothing to lose when he decided to make a run for it with two cops dangling from his car.

"He had no intention of being apprehended or caught," McCarthy told the jury. Further, McCarthy said, this was far more about politics than police work.

"The community wants someone's head. They still do," McCarthy said. "And the decision was made that someone will be served up. That was Ramiro Pena. He is the sacrificial lamb in this case."

McCarthy then posed the jury a question about Pena's handling of the case. There was no question that the officer had gotten physical with the suspect. "But ask yourself," McCarthy told the panel, "if not that, what?"

Scottie Waller never testified. Waller was behind bars on his probation violation; he opted to invoke his Fifth Amendment right against self-incrimination rather than take the stand. Germaine Taylor and the other passenger in the car disappeared; prosecutors could find neither to testify about the alleged brutality.

Instead, a parade of police officers climbed to the witness stand. Only one of them recalled seeing Pena striking Waller with a fist rather than an open hand; he changed his testimony on cross-examination.

One cop did testify that he had overheard Pena and Mandoka laughing and bragging about beating Waller in the police locker room within hours of the incident. Sgt. Mark Baker felt the comments were in "bad taste," although he acknowledged that such talk was a common way of cops blowing off steam at the end of a shift.

The other officers, called by the prosecution, seemed more like defense witnesses.

Mandoka said that after the arrest, there were "no racial comments, no laughing or disrespect. A statement like that would stick out in my mind."

Things quickly grew worse for the prosecution. Mandoka, in testimony echoed by officer Plouhar, said the county prosecutor had attempted to intimidate them into implicating Pena.

"The pressure was unbearably high," Plouhar testified. "The prosecutor's office wanted us to come up to their office, to meet and tell them what happened."

According to Mandoka, he was threatened with a perjury charge when his version of the arrest didn't jibe with what prosecutors believed had happened.

Plouhar, on cross-examination by McCarthy, acknowledged that Pena's action had likely prevented the incident from escalating. Plouhar said he had repeatedly slammed his knee into Waller's thigh in an effort to subdue the suspect, but those blows had no affect.

Officer Fellows, who was dragged the farthest by Waller's car, stormed out of the courtroom after prosecutors suggested he had tailored his story to protect Pena.

"I was asked by the prosecutor's office to speculate as to what happened," Fellows said. "I did as I was requested.... I did not lie then, nor will I start now."

The county medical examiner testified that Waller's injuries were consistent with Pena's version of the events—a series of open-hand strikes. Waller's injuries were minor at best. The prosecution case appeared to be foundering.

Muskegon Chronicle writer Michael G. Walsh, after watching week one of the trial, wrote that "little clear evidence exists that he exceeded legal limits and brutalized an African-American motorist."

McCarthy had expected to call Pena to the stand—until he saw how weak the prosecution case was. After conferring with Pena and his family, the lawyer decided not to subject his client to cross-examination. Instead, Pena's May 1997 deposition for prosecutors was read into the record. In addition to the other officers, the jury heard Pena's version of the arrest, too.

"We trimmed down what we were going to do," McCarthy said. "We just called a select number of witnesses to rebut very specific things."

One of those witnesses, Detective Dean Roesler, made it clear that this was not Waller's first go-round with police. In October 1994 Waller had fled from Roesler in his car and on foot as the detective attempted to arrest him.

"The word 'belligerent' comes to mind," Roesler told the jury. "He didn't willingly surrender and put his hands behind his back. There was a strong odor of alcohol."

This was the Scottie Waller who confronted the Muskegon police in the early morning hours of April 12, 1997.

The trial took eight days. The deliberations took two hours. The six-member jury quickly acquitted Pena because, as one alternate juror said afterward, "the prosecutor didn't prove his case at all. (Pena) did what he had to do."

Alternate juror Ruth Cross had even more to say: "If he hadn't done what he did, it could've been worse."

Pena wiped away tears once the verdict was returned, hugging and kissing his parents in the courtroom. "Emotionally, I'm beyond words," he said. "I'm very happy, appreciative. It's been a long week."

Those were Pena's last public words. He still faces an arbitration hearing in a bid to win his job back, along with Waller's civil suit. On the advice of counsel, Pena is keeping a very low profile.

His counsel, McCarthy, summed up Pena's post-trial attitude this way: "He felt singled out as a sacrificial lamb all along. I think the jury provided a response consistent with that notion."

Prosecutor Tony Tague, despite the jury's rapid repudiation of the prosecution case, defended the decision to go after Pena.

"My office did what was right, and we will stand by our decision," Tague said. The prosecutor said he intended to meet with police officials to discuss his belief that officers called by the prosecution were involved in a cover-up and may have committed perjury.

Waller had no comment on the verdict. He could not be reached at his jail cell.

## CHAPTER 6

# VOJTAS, MULHOLLAND, AND ALBERT

## *PITTSBURGH IS POLARIZED*

**THIS IS HOW QUICKLY** life changed for police Officer Michael Albert.

At 1:50 AM on October 12, 1995, he was on routine patrol, monitoring his police radio, enjoying a quiet shift in the sleepy Pittsburgh suburb of Baldwin Borough. The reverie was interrupted by a voice coming across the radio—a cop in a neighboring town announcing a traffic stop and requesting backup.

With nothing else to do, Albert decided to ride over and help. He arrived at 1:56 AM to find a brawl under way between the car's driver and three police officers. He joined in the fray.

At 1:59 AM, he radioed to headquarters that they needed leg restraints to control the combative suspect. He had been on the scene only three minutes, a scant 180 seconds.

At 2:11 AM, the suspect went into cardiac arrest after a wild fight which ended when officers—five were at the scene, and they were in and out of the scuffle—were finally able to subdue him. Three minutes later, unaware that the suspect would die, Officer Michael Albert returned to finish his shift on the streets of Baldwin.

At 3:06 AM, the car's driver was pronounced dead at Mercy Hospital. Michael Albert wouldn't find out until later, but just 86 minutes after he answered the call to provide backup on a traffic stop, he became a murder suspect. So did the cop who radioed for backup, Lt. Milton Mulholland, and another policeman who provided backup, Officer John Vojtas.

The driver, it turned out, was a black man. The arresting officers, on whose watch the driver had died,

> Another trial date would have to be scheduled. The two policemen were learning a lot about the old legal saw that "justice delayed is justice denied."

were all white men. Controversy was quick to follow, to land smack dab in the middle of the three cops' ordinarily mundane lives.

It took only eighty-six minutes to go from law enforcers to suspects, from cops to alleged killers.

Eighty-six minutes. It was long enough to change Michael Albert's life.

The death of the car's driver, thirty-one-year-old Jonny E. Gammage, drew national attention, prompted comment from the Rev. Jesse Jackson, and created racial tensions in the city of Pittsburgh. One of the few facts in the case that everyone agrees on—and one of the reasons this death almost instantly became such a major issue—is that Gammage was the cousin of then-Pittsburgh Steelers defensive lineman Ray Seals.

Gammage and Seals were more than relatives, they were lifelong friends who considered themselves brothers. Their mothers were sisters, and the cousins grew up together in Syracuse. Seals never attended college, the traditional path to the National Football League, but played semi-pro football while he worked as a hotel doorman. Although others wondered if Seals would ever achieve his goal of playing professionally, Gammage constantly supported his cousin, urging him not to give in or give up.

**The group that slandered the officer's good name was later exposed as a wholesaler of heroin and cocaine.**

Seals, the ex-linebacker for the Syracuse Express of the Eastern Football League, made it in 1989. He signed a contract with the Tampa Bay Buccaneers. Five years later, he signed with the Pittsburgh Steelers. After moving to western Pennsylvania, he invited Gammage to join him in Pittsburgh. The cousins launched a news sportswear line— "60 Minute Men"—with a portion of the proceeds designated for charity. The pair had grown up with a healthy respect for the law; Seals's father was a thirty-year veteran of the Syracuse police department.

Brentwood police Lt. Milton Mulholland knew none of this in the early morning of October 12, 1995, when he stopped a dark blue Jaguar with Florida plates heading north on Route 51 in the Pittsburgh suburbs. The Jaguar had tinted windows, making it hard to see inside. Mulholland said the car was driving erratically, and it was later determined that problems with the car's brake pads may have caused its driver to repeatedly tap the brakes. The flashing brake lights were enough to capture the lieutenant's attention.

It was that ultimate police oxymoron—the routine vehicle stop. The request for license and registration doesn't always turn out to be routine. Anything can happen, and it often does.

It did this night.

**What if the officers had simply been doing what they were trained to do, and Jonny Gammage died anyway?**

Mulholland, fifty-seven, was a twenty-year police veteran on the night that he stopped Jonny Gammage's sports car. He immediately called for backup, even before his patrol car had rolled to a stop. Officer John Vojtas of the Brentwood police responded, as did Officer Michael Albert of the neighboring Baldwin police. Two other officers arrived as well—Officer Shawn Patterson and Sgt. Keith Henderson of the Whitehall PD.

Mulholland was in his vehicle, calling in the license plate, when his backup arrived. The officers ordered the driver to exit the vehicle with his hands up and empty. Vojtas approached the car and began speaking with Gammage. When he told the driver to get out of the car, Gammage exited with a cellular phone in one hand, the officers said later. Vojtas, believing it might be a weapon, told Gammage to put it down. The officers said Gammage ignored their instructions; Vojtas wound up using his police flashlight to smack the cellular phone out of Gammage's hand. Almost instantly, a struggle was under way.

Patterson, testifying later, said it escalated quickly. "Everyone was screaming orders at Mr. Gammage," he said. "...[h]e is responding violently, trying to strike all the officers."

Henderson later recalled it this way: Gammage emerged holding something that appeared to be a gun. Vojtas's eyes widened in surprise and fear, and the officer swung his flashlight at Gammage. The driver then attacked Vojtas. Henderson said he had his weapon pulled at this time.

Three police officers, three stories, all agreed on the main point: Gammage was the instigator. There was never any evidence introduced that the three had an opportunity to collaborate on their stories, to make them jibe; the officers worked for different departments in different jurisdictions. Vojtas, after receiving treatment at a local hospital, filled out his report at the request of Brentwood Police Chief Wayne Babish.

Gammage's family, in a civil suit, presented their version of what happened that night.

After Vojtas struck the cellular phone, Gammage grabbed the officer's flashlight. A second officer, Henderson, came to Vojtas's aid. Vojtas slammed Gammage against the car with Henderson's help. Mulholland jumped in, helping the other two force Gammage to the ground. Vojtas then smashed Gammage in the face, while Henderson swung his flashlight into Gammage's right thigh.

With Gammage now face down and beaten, Albert arrived, as did Patterson, and the five officers kept applying pressure on the prone suspect until he finally died.

The officers told a different story. To the five officers, Gammage was not a victim. Gammage was an out-of-control wild man who battled five cops, biting one of their thumbs almost to the bone, a suspect who never stopped kicking and punching until he was finally held down with restraints. At one point during the brawl, one officer recalled, Gammage mimicked the battling officers by calling out their first names—his impersonation of their calls for assistance from backups.

It was then, after the fighting was over, that the 5-foot-7, 187-pound Gammage went into cardiac arrest and stopped breathing.

The report filed by the thirty-two-year-old Albert following the incident detailed what was going on when he arrived just six minutes after Mulholland had decided to pull the Jaguar over. "It was immediately apparent that a violent altercation was taking place," he wrote. One handcuff was dangling from Gammage's wrist, and the suspect was fighting—somewhat successfully—against three officers.

An exhausted Mulholland, upon seeing Albert, stumbled away from the fray. "Get in there, Mike," he told the younger cop. "I've had enough. I can't take it."

Albert said that Gammage was briefly face down, kicking at the arresting officers, but then reared back up on his knees and clamped his teeth down on Vojtas's thumb, biting through nearly to the bone. At this, Albert used his police baton to put pressure on Gammage's shoulder and neck, trying to force the suspect to let go of Vojtas' thumb. Once that happened, Gammage reared up again. Albert then used his foot and knee on Gammage's neck and shoulder to subdue him before heading over to assist the injured Vojtas.

Albert had arrived, according to police logs, at 1:56 AM. At 1:58 AM, he went back to his police car to get restraints for Gammage, who was still battling wildly with Henderson and Patterson. In a radio call, Albert told the dispatcher, "Hey, I'm backing Whitehall. They got a fight going on down here at 51 and Overbrook. Do you have any flexicuffs?"

A short time later, he made it clear what was going on at the scene: "If you can, put a push on it. It took about four (officers) to take this guy down." The comment, made in the middle of the fray, seemed to lend credence to the reports filed later by the officers.

People who arrived late in the incident—a medic, other police officers—said Gammage was still kicking at police when they hit the scene. A Pittsburgh police officer recalled that even after three officers put the restraints on Gammage's legs, the suspect kept on struggling.

Albert noted in his report on the incident that when Gammage was finally subdued, "everyone seemed exhausted." Thirty to forty seconds later, a Brentwood medic yelled that Gammage was "going into arrest!" As Gammage collapsed, Vojtas—his badly damaged thumb still bleeding—was worried that the suspect could have infected him with the HIV virus. "If I die," he snapped angrily, "I hope he dies."

Jonny Gammage did die. And Vojtas, along with Albert and Mulholland, would be charged in his death following an emotional, racially-charged investigation.

Before any charges were filed, before any investigation was completed, the Rev. Jesse Jackson was comparing the Gammage death to an old-fashioned "lynching," as if the

KKK had stopped him and thrown a rope over a tree along-side Route 51.

Given the connection to professional sports and the racial angle, Gammage's death created an instant national furor. Political pressure was heavy for authorities to do some-thing—mostly arrest the five cops involved. The cops sud-denly found a disturbing lack of official support, with the police commissioner and the mayor now distancing them-selves from their officers—a fairly standard move in such cases. The pressure increased after a coroner's jury recom-mended homicide charges against the five on November 4, 1995. A forensic pathologist had told the jury that there were twenty cuts, bruises, and scrapes on Gammage's body. The cause of death for Gammage was officially listed as positional asphyxiation. Translation: Gammage had suffocated against the pavement when he was held down by the arresting offi-cers, who most likely used their knees or batons.

Although he had battled five police officers for at least five minutes, Gammage had no broken bones or any major internal injuries.

The case moved to the district attorney's office. Allegheny County prosecutor Robert Colville was the former Pittsburgh police chief, now serving his sixth four-year term as district attorney.

Colville stood up on November 27, 1995, and announced he was charging Mulholland and Vojtas with murder, invol-untary manslaughter, and official oppression. Albert was charged with involuntary manslaughter.

Henderson was not charged; the prosecutor called him "a necessary and essential witness for the successful prosecution of the other three officers." Patterson was not charged or relied upon as a witness; a source, speaking on condition of anonymity, suggested the decision to let him walk was linked to the officer's family ties.

Patterson's father was a Pittsburgh police commander. The Pittsburgh police were handling the Gammage investigation.

His statement in announcing the charges showed that Colville was walking a thin line: satisfying Gammage's backers without alienating law enforcement personnel.

"I recognize and appreciate the tragic loss suffered by the Gammage family and the community interests which Jon Gammage's death represent," he said. "I am also fully cognizant of the difficult and dangerous task police officers take every day."

Vojtas's lawyer, James M. Ecker, raised a point that nobody else had touched on: What if the officers had simply been doing what they were trained to do, and Jonny Gammage died anyway? "I don't think they did anything dramatically different," Ecker said, "from what they were taught."

Officer Vojtas was represented at his trial by two attorneys, Ecker and Alexander Lindsay. In doing their homework on the case, the pair discovered the truth was somewhat different from "the mythology which surrounds this case." The mythology—half-truths, oft-repeated rumors, downright inaccuracies—seemed to have a life of its own, but little to do with what actually happened. The two attorneys wound up writing a newspaper article to set the record straight, detailing the myths and presenting their rebuttals:

MYTH: A white cop pulled over a motorist because the man was black and driving through a white neighborhood.

FACT: There was no evidence that Mulholland knew Gammage was black. It was nighttime and the car had tinted windows. Unless Gammage rolled down the window, it was impossible to see inside. And while Brentwood is a predominantly white town, the traffic stop occurred on a four-lane highway—hardly a privileged white enclave.

MYTH: White cops gave the outnumbered black man a beating for no reason.

FACT: Testimony indicated that Henderson hit Gammage on the legs only after the driver had first kicked at him and punched Vojtas. Vojtas testified at the coroner's inquest that he punched Gammage only after he was bitten on the thumb.

MYTH: The officers sat on top of Gammage until he suffocated.

FACT: The defense challenged the prosecution to point to any evidence whatsoever that five police officers ever got on top of Gammage and held him to the pavement for any sustained period of time. This challenge went unanswered by the prosecution.

MYTH: This was a routine traffic stop.

FACT: Once Gammage began resisting arrest, "there was nothing routine about this traffic stop."

MYTH: An all-white jury acquitted Vojtas because he, too, was white.

FACT: The evidence simply did not back up the charges.

"If you read the editorials, it always came back to this: Five police officers got on top of Jonny Gammage and held him down," Lindsay said. "That just didn't happen. When I'm talking about the mythology, that's what I mean."

In January 1996, the Steelers and Ray Seals made the Super Bowl. While his teammates like Rod Woodson and Neil O'Donnell answered questions about game plans and zone blitzes, Seals was asked repeatedly by reporters about his late cousin.

"I want to be overwhelmed and real happy about going to the Super Bowl," Seals told his questioners. "But at the same time there's a part that's just 'Swoosh!' because my cousin isn't going to be a part of it. I can imagine how happy he'd be."

The officers, under a gag order, were legally barred from telling their story to the public or the press.

Before there were any trials—and there would be three, with at least one more still to come—the charges against the three cops would change. Allegheny County Court Judge James McGregor, ruling that the prosecution had never demonstrated that the officers intended to kill Gammage, threw out the murder charges against Vojtas and Mulholland. He tossed the official oppression charge as well, saying Mulholland had not acted illegally when he stopped Gammage's car that October night. The evidence against the cops was simply insufficient to support that serious charge recommended by Collville.

Votjas, who had suffered the severe bite wound from Gammage, was granted a separate trial from the other two because he planned to claim self-defense. Vojtas, a former

Marine who had custody of his two children, was particularly upset by the pre-trial publicity about the case.

"I think I'm being painted as a monster, and I'm not a monster," said the fifteen-year police veteran. Vojtas described himself as "a good, hard-working cop."

Ten months after the McGregor ruling, on October 15, 1996, Mulholland and Albert became the first officers to go on trial for killing Gammage. It promised to be a contentious case, and the jury was selected from suburban Philadelphia to cut down the chances of pre-trial contamination by the massive publicity in the Pittsburgh area.

Both Mulholland and Albert were facing five years in prison if convicted of involuntary manslaughter in the case.

The court was filled with supporters of the Gammage family, and protesters gathered outside virtually every day. Friends of the officers, while outnumbered, appeared as well. One Brentwood resident said that Mulholland was "one of the most stand-up guys you'll ever meet."

The courtroom crowd, pro or con, meant little to the defense, which planned a twofold attack: They would combat the emotional nature of Gammage's death with experts who would testify that the officers had acted appropriately and that asphyxiation was only a possible cause of death.

They had also uncovered information that Gammage had grown violent during previous traffic stops in Syracuse—one nine months before his death, the other four months earlier. In one case, defense attorneys asserted, Gammage had become angry and physical with one officer. Defense lawyers wanted to let the two Syracuse police officers involved testify about Gammage's past conduct.

"In each case, Gammage became the aggressor," wrote defense attorney Lindsay. "Specifically, Gammage's habit was to try to take over the situation, become verbally abusive with the police officers and ultimately physically confronting them."

The officers were not permitted to testify. Judge David R. Cashman said the previous incidents failed to establish a pattern of conduct by Gammage.

The attack on the asphyxiation finding was at odds with the autopsies conducted by county pathologist Dr. Al Shakir and of now-Allegheny County coroner Wecht, who was hired by Ray Seals as an independent pathologist to conduct a second autopsy on Gammage. Wecht subsequently became the county coroner.

Shakir had found that the autopsy was inconclusive as to cause of death, but said that additional testimony from a coroner's inquest had convinced him this was a homicide. Were Mulholland and Albert responsible for this death? "I don't think it's my duty to sort out who did what," Shakir said. The officers' actions "as a whole" led to the death. But only two of the officers were on trial; only three were ever accused. The defense was convinced this was evidence of selective prosecution.

When he took the stand on the third day of testimony, Wecht said that he had determined that Gammage died while lying prone with his hands behind his back.

He was one of the government's star witnesses, a man who had performed more than 12,000 autopsies, including one on Waco, Texas, cult leader David Koresh.

Mulholland's lawyer, Patrick J. Thomassey, was grilling the coroner during cross-examination to explain exactly what role his client had played in Gammage's death. "You tell me what my client did. Tell me what my client did from A to Z," Thomassey challenged.

"It's not for me to tell you what your client did," Wecht responded. "It's for the client to tell me, the ladies and gentlemen of the jury, what he did, what he was doing there, and why he was participating in this."

Mulholland, of course, had no obligation to testify at all in the case; judges routinely instruct juries that the decision by a defendant not to testify does not infer anything because of their Fifth Amendment right against self-incrimation. Yet here was Wecht, in front of the jury, demanding that Mulholland do just that.

Thomassey demanded—and was granted—a mistrial.

"I am so personally affronted by what (Wecht) did," Thomassey fumed outside the courtroom. "I think it's almost intentional."

Another trial date would have to be scheduled. The two policemen were learning a lot about the old legal saw that "justice delayed is justice denied."

After the mistrial, Judge Cashman was vilified for his handling of the case—specifically, for arranging for the jurors in the mistral to meet with attorneys in the case from both sides. The defense had taken him up on the suggestion, while the prosecution had not. Two jurors, after meeting the defense attorneys, thought that Cashman was demonstrating a bias toward the police officers. Others jurors disagreed, backing up Cashman's claim that he had invited both sides.

Critics demanded that Cashman recuse himself because of his preferential treatment of the defense. Cashman was outraged.

"If I were to recuse myself, then I would have to say that I did something wrong, and I could not go forward because I did something wrong," Cashman said. "Well let me assure you, ladies and gentlemen, I did nothing wrong."

The prosecution, echoing complaints from the NAACP and other groups, disagreed. Prosecutor Michael Streily told the judge "there is a frank public community perception that his honor has lost his ability to impartially preside over the trial."

Thomassey, in rebutting Streily's claim, complained that "the inmates are running the asylum." He asked Cashman to stay on the case even though "you have not given us one rul-ing.... This case has become a joke. I'm asking you to grab everybody by the throat and say we're going to go try this case.... We don't care what the public perception is, because you didn't do anything wrong."

Cashman eventually agreed, and stayed on to preside over the cases.

"Do we let the lions and the Christians in the Coliseum put their thumbs up and thumbs down, or do we look to the length of Madame LaFarge's knitting to make a determina-tion as to how justice should be handled?" he asked rhetori-cally about the flap over his impartiality.

John Vojtas went on trial on November 4, 1996, with a jury culled from another Philadelphia suburb. Even there, it wasn't easy to find unbiased jurors; one black woman was released after saying she was convinced by news reports that the officer had killed Gammage.

Vojtas, like Albert and Mulholland before him, was looking at a five-year jail term if convicted.

"My client was scared," defense attorney Lindsay recently reflected. "He was charged with a serious crime. He was concerned that somehow the jury would be working on a different wave length."

One of the first prosecution witnesses was Ray Seals, who had played for the Steelers in the Super Bowl ten months earlier. The other witnesses were not as reliable.

There was Frank Belejac, a tow-truck driver who initially told police that he had seen nothing before suddenly changing his mind. Belejac had other problems besides his evolving story; he had suffered a brain aneurysm in 1988 that had affected his memory. No witnesses presented any information alleging that race played any role in the fight between Gammage and the police.

Shakir, who performed the official autopsy on Gammage, again acknowledged that he could not make the official determination of a homicide based strictly on the dead man's external injuries. Lindsay said that Shakir's conclusion was based on the injuries plus information provided by a Pittsburgh city police commander who said that five police officers had climbed on top of Gammage and held him down. Shakir never spoke with any of the officers at the scene for their version. The police commander was not called to testify at the trial.

Lindsay was somewhat stunned by the whole exchange.

"I don't know that this commander ever said that," Lindsay said. "And in any event, none of the witnesses ever corroborated that."

For the first time, jurors heard a different theory of how Gammage died. Seattle Medical Examiner Dr. Donald Reay said he would have classified Gammage's death as an accident rather than a homicide. According to Reay, the cause of death could have been accidental restraint asphyxia. Gammage could have stopped breathing when officers tried to restrain him during the brawl outside his car, Reay said. Without knowing exactly how long the officers had been on top of Gammage, it was impossible to call this a homicide, Reay said.

Lindsay, in his opening statement, had suggested exhaustion or an adrenaline rush as other possible causes of death. If one of those scenarios had occurred, "there (are) no clues," he told the jury. "In other words, if you drop dead from exhaustion, if... you get scared to death and you go into cardiac arrest from adrenaline... there will be no clues left in your body."

The defense created a timeline for the case, using the radio transmissions between the police cars. It was clear when Albert had radioed for medial assistance for Vojtas— 2:03 AM. Gammage did not die for at least another eight minutes, and Vojtas—his thumb in bad, bad shape—never re-entered the fight once he was bitten. The officer had also suffered a knee injury and a chipped elbow in his fight to subdue Gammage.

The defense then produced an expert witness, Robert C. Willis, who unveiled a series of James Bond-ish weapons that looked like ordinary products from everyday life. His point: Gammage's cellular phone appeared much more dangerous to a police officer familiar with such weaponry. Willis produced a potentially lethal beeper and ballpoint pen.

The defense rested, the case wrapped up, and the jurors began deliberating. Lindsay remembered his thoughts as the panel went out.

"If you read the news accounts, you could not help but get the impression it was a very close trial," the attorney said. "But the trial I was attending was a blowout. It was 50-0, and we were still in the third quarter. The night the jury went out, I was thinking one thought: Ain't no way possibly they could convict on this evidence.

"My only concern was that the public was going to be surprised, because unlike the jury, they didn't sit through the trial."

Lindsay, in additional to being a good lawyer, isn't half bad as a prognosticator. He was right on both points: Vojtas was acquitted after fifteen hours of deliberations over three days. And people who were unfamiliar with the evidence, with what had happened in the courtroom, expressed knee-jerk outrage over the verdict.

The jury was unapologetic about the verdict. The first people to actually hear the evidence, to sift through the radio transmissions and the eyewitness testimony, to consider only what had happened that night, had come to the conclusion that Officer John Vojtas was innocent. The jury had visited the site where Belejac testified that he had stood and watched the brawl; from there, it was impossible to get a clear view of where the fight occurred.

"There was much reasonable doubt," offered the jury foreman, speaking on condition of anonymity. Another juror, thirty-eight-year-old Carol Sobolewski of Scranton, defended the verdict.

"I know the people in Pittsburgh are quite upset with us, but we were fair," she said afterward. "This policeman, in his duties, did nothing wrong."

Nothing wrong? What about the racial overtones? Sobolewski said that based on the evidence, there were none.

"If it was the opposite, it Mr. Vojtas was black and Mr. Gammage was white, we would have come back with the same verdict," she said. The foreman echoed her comments: "None of us at all, in any shape or form, are racist."

A third juror, also speaking on condition of anonymity, said race was actually a red herring in this case. "It didn't matter what color this victim was," the juror said. "He could have been purple."

Vojtas, after months of public flogging, wept in the courtroom after the verdict was announced. He was solemn rather than celebratory; leaving the courthouse, his first comment was simply "Praise the Lord."

"I'm sorry that a tragic accident happened last year," he said. "I know I'm going to learn from this.… I hope that other policemen in our department and surrounding areas—in fact, the world—can learn from this tragic accident and that this thing will never happen again."

Despite constant comparison between the Gammage case and the Rodney King case, there was hardly any violence or rioting in Pittsburgh following the acquittal. A minor flareup between protesting high school students and a sporting goods store—no injuries, no property damage—was the only incident linked to the verdict.

The acquittal did not come without cost to Vojtas. His legal bills climbed well into six figures, a tough nut for a married cop with kids. And though the jurors said he was not responsible for the death of Jonny Gammage, their verdict did little to change the opinions of many who had not spent a single minute of the nine-day trial listening to the testimony.

"I think justice could have been done better," said Pittsburgh Mayor Tom Murphy.

Gammage's girlfriend, Jean Leflore, condemned Vojtas as "a murderer" who "beat (Gammage) like a dog." The Pittsburgh Post-Gazette, in a post-verdict editorial, was not as harsh, but still proved damning to Vojtas.

The verdict did not "exonerate Officer Vojtas," the editorial opined. "The foreman may have said… 'not guilty,' but this seemed closer to the old Scottish verdict of 'not proven.' Jonny Gammage died; that is a blot upon Officer Vojtas no matter what."

Vojtas was able to get his job back, and get his life back in some kind of order. He was eventually promoted to sergeant. But the case hung over his former co-defendants like a sword of Damocles. Albert remained in a state of limbo at work, stuck on administrative duty. Mulholland had retired from the Brentwood police, and was working as a janitor in the Pittsburgh school system.

Suddenly, in April 1997, Judge Cashman dropped the charges against Mulholland and Albert in a sharply-worded decision.

"When one acknowledges the fact... that these individuals were the only ones prosecuted, it becomes clear that a political purpose was attempting to be served rather than the interest of justice," Cashman ruled. Mulholland and Albert received a reprieve—but it lasted just six months.

Nearly two years to the day after Gammage's death, the Pennsylvania Supreme Court overruled that decision and ordered a retrial. The nightmare was not over for Mulholland, now fifty-eight, and Albert, now thirty-three.

In November 1997 Gammage's parents went to Washington and called on Attorney General Janet Reno to consider federal civil rights charges against the officers at the scene of their son's death. The Vojtas verdict was an afterthought as they issued their emotional plea. The upcoming trial of the other two officers, and the possibly prejudicial effect their comments could have, were not considered.

"You must put the constitution above your own personal belief," Narves Gammage, the dead man's mother, said in her message to Reno. "To restore my faith, you must act now."

Two weeks later, Mulholland and Albert were back in a Pittsburgh courtroom for their second trial on involuntary manslaughter charges. The defense lawyers, in their opening statements, offered some new explanations for what happened that night. Why was Gammage so irate? He feared that the $5 bag of marijuana inside his cousin's car would be a public relations nightmare.

"I would suggest to you that Mr. Gammage got this nickel bag of dope," Thomassey said. "He is going down Route 51, and Milt Mulholland gets behind him, and he is thinking, 'What am I going to do now? If they search this car and find this and make this connection with Ray Seals as my cousin, what am I going to do?'"

Albert's lawyer, Thomas Ceraso, mentioned that Gammage had a history of heart problems—another point that had previously never been mentioned.

Belejac testified again for the prosecution, as did a twice-convicted burglar who admitted that he was "pretty high" on beer when he drove past the scene. Car salesman Dennis Mazon also acknowledged that he was taking anti-depressant medication that night, and that he initially thought the incident occurred around 9:30 PM on October 11—more than four hours before it actually happened. He added that one of his burglary arrests resulted from Mulholland's police work, but insisted that had nothing to do with his testimony.

For the first time in any of the three trials, a witness testified about racial prejudice. A security guard at a local park testified that Mulholland had once told him that he would stop "any niggers driving a new car." It was a potentially explosive charge; unfortunately, Thomas Bates had never used that incendiary word when initially telling the district attorney's office about his encounter with Mulholland.

Thomassey subsequently produced fifty-eight "arrest cards" that listed traffic stops made by Mulholland in the twenty months before Gammage's death. Fifty-seven of the people stopped were white; just a single driver was black. No one was called to corroborate Bates's testimony, or to offer other examples of Mulholland's "racism."

The defense team was again blocked from introducing testimony about Gammage's previous police stops in Syracuse. In the first stop, he allegedly ignored an officer's orders to get out of the car. When Gammage finally did exit the vehicle, he was kicking dirt, yelling, and swearing. The officer said he felt threatened.

Seven months later, he reportedly shoved a police officer after getting pulled over. According to the cop involved, Gammage was given a ticket and released after invoking the name of his uncle, the veteran Syracuse policeman.

The jury did hear from the coroner, Dr. Shakir. Under questioning from the defense, he said yes, it was impossible to say whether the two officers sitting at the defense table had killed Gammage.

"Only God knows," Shakir said.

The defense called Dr. Reay, who again disputed Shakir's ruling of a homicide. A recess was declared during his testimony when protesters' chants of "No justice, no peace" began wafting through the courtroom.

Jeffrey Sheldon, an instructor at the Allegheny County Sheriff's Department, testified that the techniques used by the officers to subdue Gammage were the same ones they had taught to law enforcement officers for more than a quarter-century.

Pittsburgh police Officer Regis Lattner, from the witness stand, painted Mulholland in a far different light than prosecutors did. When he arrived at the scene, Mulholland was in such bad shape that Lattner's first question was, "Are you shot?"

Mulholland was "pale white, like ready to collapse, like maybe have a heart attack or something," Lattner recalled. "Ashen color. Pale looking."

Describing Gammage in a radio call to his base, Lattner offered four words: "Guy's a wild man." And he recalled Mulholland's first words to him: "Help those guys cuff him. He's out of control."

In his closing argument, Assistant District Attorney Edward Borkowski told the jury, "This was a man knocked to the ground, pinned to the ground, pressed and restricted until he died."

Thomassey gave the panel a cop's eye view of what happened: "He was kicking the hell out of five officers.... If we can't enforce the law, we have the Wild West."

The jury retired to deliberate. Eleven of them were soon convinced that the officers were innocent. There was one holdout—the panel's lone black member, fifty-three-year-old Walter Moorefield. For the second time, there was a mistrial. Once again, there was no closure for Mulholland or Albert.

Albert fought back tears when the mistrial was declared. "Our clients are upset," said his lawyer, Ceraso. "They want the case over."

Thomassey said he believed peer pressure in the black community had forced Moorefield to hold out against an acquittal. The lone holdout had told his fellow jurors they could discuss and deliberate "until doomsday" and he would not change his mind.

"I wouldn't want to be that poor juror, because people don't come to the courtroom, people don't listen to the evidence," Thomassey said. "They just know that unfortunately a black motorist is killed, it's at the hands of white police, so something must be wrong.

"It must have something to do with race. And it didn't."

One of the white jurors told a local television station that everyone except Moorefield had reached the conclusion that the officers were not guilty.

"In the end, all the facts pretty much (came) together, and I thought it was fairly easy to see the truth," the juror said. "I thought the truth was that it was a tragedy, an accident, a bad situation that just got out of hand and went bad."

Moorefield had also told some jurors that he feared a backlash in the black community if he voted to acquit. "Walter said something to the effect that the organizations he belongs to, he would have to go back and answer to them," said jury forewoman June Gaspar. "He was serious. The ones of us who heard him say that did not think it was a flip comment."

Moorefield was taking Thorazine during the trial to combat his hiccups. The drug made him drowsy, and he occasionally nodded off during the testimony despite the efforts of fellow jurors to keep him alert. Gaspar said that was one of the things that bothered her about the deliberations.

"We had to make a decision about two men's lives," she said. "We had only 98 percent participation on the jury. The whole experience was frustrating. We had a person who wouldn't listen to reason."

In a strange but telling twist, the jurors collected money to present to court staffers who had helped them during the trial. When the staff declined to accept it, the jurors decided to give the money to Mulholland instead.

The accused cop donated the money to charity.

The defense lawyers pressed for the charges to be dropped, saying another trial—a third trial—would be double jeopardy. Superior Court Senior Judge James Rowley, who had presided over the second trial, declined to dismiss the charges against Mulholland and Albert. The decision on whether to prosecute the pair again would rest with the new Allegheny district attorney, Stephen Zappala, Jr., who had replaced veteran prosecutor Colville.

Zappala's decision: Trial No. 3 would be held. "I am convinced a unanimous decision can be reached in this matter," said the prosecutor, ignoring the fact that one nearly had been reached—one for acquittal—just a month before. The bill for trying these three officers, already at $146,213 in expenses just for the cost of the juries, would continue to climb.

Thomassey attacked the decision, but this time he found that some people were agreeing with him. Duquesne University law professor Kenneth Hirsch echoed Thomassey's criticism.

"I think someone with more time in office and someone more politically secure... would have held a press conference and said, 'We understand the grief of the Gammage family, but we don't have the evidence to convict these officers,'" Hirsch said.

Zappala disagreed. Former Lt. Milton Mulholland and Officer Michael Albert are awaiting their third trial in the death of Jonny Gammage—and they have at least one more trial awaiting once that is finished. The Gammage family's civil suit is expected to start winding its way through the legal system once the criminal cases are finally wrapped up.

*Chapter 7*

# BLAKE HUBBARD

## *WHEN DO YOU SHOOT?*

**HE'S THOUGHT ABOUT WHAT HAPPENED** a million times. A day rarely passes when it doesn't cross his mind. He can recite every detail of what happened that afternoon, from the first call crackling across his police radio, to his arrival on the scene, to the moment when he made the decision to fire his weapon.

Blake Hubbard will politely spend fifteen, twenty minutes discussing the nearly sixty seconds where he faced the moment that he never thought would arrive.

Hubbard, a fourth-generation law enforcer who plied the family trade with the Grand Prairie Police Department down in Texas, was just going to back up a fellow officer that day in this southern town, population 99,606. It was not the kind of place where a police officer often had cause to fire his weapon; even if he did, it was not the kind of place where the locals ordinarily objected to a police officer doing his job.

What strikes Blake Hubbard most of all about that day is how fast everything changed on October 7, 1996.

"Less than a minute," he says now, looking back on that day. "Less than a minute. My involvement in this situation was less than a minute."

In those sixty seconds, Hubbard arrived at a vacant lot bordered by a chain link fence. He found fellow police officer Barry Fletcher in a standoff with a suspect who had a history of mental illness, a man by the name of Joseph Lee Calloway. Calloway, a schizophrenic who lived on the streets, had a knife. Fletcher, who had less experience on the job than the twenty-seven-year-old Hubbard, ordered Calloway to drop his knife, but to no avail. He then tried to disarm him with a telescoping baton and pepper spray.

> It was that ultimate police oxymoron—the routine vehicle stop. The request for license and registration doesn't always turn out to be routine. Anything can happen, and it often does.

Nothing worked. And when, for the third time, Calloway took a swipe at Fletcher with his knife, Hubbard pulled the trigger to save his partner's life. He fired twice into Calloway's chest. Calloway was dead at the scene.

"I really didn't expect it would ever go that far," Hubbard says now, months later, his life inexorably altered by that single encounter. "I've been in that situation before. The suspect always puts the knife down once you draw your weapon. I figured this one would be the same way."

It wasn't. And after one minute in a vacant lot in a small town in Texas, Blake Hubbard found everything was different. His co-workers brought him in for fingerprinting and mug shots. His bosses turned their backs on him. Strangers were suddenly maligning him. People were calling him a killer and a racist. He was out of work, with mounting legal bills, looking at a murder charge and some hard jail time.

The local chapter of the NAACP had targeted Hubbard, even though nobody —not even the eyewitnesses who questioned his judgment—suggested that he had pulled the trigger because of any racial factor. But the politics of race was nevertheless the deciding factor in the Hubbard case. It suddenly became a familiar story: white cop... black victim. It had to be racial, regardless of the circumstances, the variables, the facts. Regardless of what happened, what Hubbard had to say.

There was one other twist: Fletcher, the officer whose life was saved when Hubbard pulled the trigger, filed a report indicating that Hubbard had no reason to shoot that afternoon. Only later did Fletcher claim that he had been coerced into selling out his co-worker.

Hubbard was, in short order, fired from his job and indicted for murder.

"I've defended outlaws on the street who killed people in cold blood who were treated better than this," said John Read, the savvy defense attorney who wound up representing Hubbard. In the days after the indictment, "I had fourteen or fifteen calls from police officers," Read said. "This is very tough on them, because when you throw handcuffs on a police officer, crimes are going to go up."

It was tougher on Hubbard than anyone else. Blake Hubbard had trouble understanding what had happened, and how it had happened so fast. But he soon came to know one thing: If he didn't fight for himself, nobody else would.

Typically, it was not a bizarre or extraordinary call that ended Joseph Lee Calloway's life and forever changed Hubbard's. Hubbard was on regular patrol that day, cruising through Grand Prairie. It was dull, it was routine, it was usually unexciting—and Blake Hubbard loved absolutely every minute of it.

Law enforcement blood coursed through the veins of this young man, who had put in two years on the Grand Prairie PD. His grandfather and great-grandfather on his mother's side had worked as U.S. Customs agents. His dad had been a deputy sheriff in Texas. As a kid, Hubbard could not imagine going into any other line of work.

> "It wasn't a factor. I felt that if the guy I shot was a white guy, or if I was a black cop, this wouldn't be happening."

"I loved it, yeah," he said fourteen months after the incident that took his livelihood away. "It was great. I loved so many things about it. I liked the fact that it was an outside job. I loved the excitement. I loved the ability to help people. I loved the satisfaction of catching the bad guy, the lawbreaker, and putting him in jail. I loved the job."

The person who needed help on October 7 turned out to be a fellow police officer, a relatively new man on the force named Fletcher. He had less than two years on the job when he and Hubbard took to their streets in their uniforms and patrol cars.

It was about 5 PM when Fletcher answered the call—a report of an emotionally disturbed person in the 2000 block of Sherman Street, in a predominantly black Grand Prairie neighborhood known as Dalworth. It was the town's highest-crime area, known among the local police for the prevalence of street crime and prostitution. When Fletcher arrived, summoned by someone in the neighborhood, he saw Calloway, fifty-two, alternately talking to himself and yelling at passing motorists. Calloway, nicknamed "Uncle Joe" by neighborhood residents used to his rambling presence on the block, was known to police as a man with mental problems. He was also waving a four-inch pocketknife.

Fletcher attempted to handle the situation himself, shouting at Calloway to drop the knife and so end the incident. But Calloway ignored his repeated entreaties to surrender the weapon, and continued his irrational behavior. The officer then fired a blast of pepper spray at Calloway, but he appeared immune to the noxious mixture and went on waving the knife and rambling.

At this point, Fletcher decided that he needed some backup. He called the dispatcher, who sent Hubbard out to assist his fellow officer. Hubbard still remembers that the call, though nothing he hadn't handled before, carried a certain sense of urgency.

"I knew it had a high-risk element," Hubbard remembers. "An officer on the scene by himself. A suspect with a knife."

But then again, it seemed to be rather tame. The suspect's knife was a folding knife, and it was closed. And the suspect was backing away, rather than confronting, the officer on the scene. Hubbard drove to the scene without his lights or siren going—but his "sixth sense" still told him that something was going on.

He was right. Things had changed rather dramatically by the time Hubbard made it over to Sherman Street.

Hubbard spotted Fletcher's patrol car and stopped behind it, but his fellow officer was nowhere in sight. The suspect had moved a few blocks away. His knife was now open, and he was waving it at Fletcher. Hubbard, seeing and hearing the commotion down the street, ran to the scene, where he saw Fletcher in a standoff with the suspect.

Fletcher was shouting at Calloway to drop the knife. He screamed it over and over—"Drop the fucking knife!"—so often that Hubbard can't even remember how many times those four words were shouted. However many times, Calloway didn't acknowledge them even once. His bizarre behavior continued.

At this point, Fletcher and Calloway started a deadly dance. The officer had his gun in his left hand and his telescoping baton in his right hand. Fletcher extended his baton and moved closer to smack the knife out of Calloway's hand. With each swing at Calloway's wrist, Fletcher moved closer into harm's way. With each swing, Calloway showed no sign of dropping the weapon. It happened once. It happened twice. When it happened a third time, and Hubbard made his decision.

"On the third time, the suspect raised the knife and tried to move toward Fletcher," Hubbard recalls. "At that point, I felt Officer Fletcher's life was in danger."

It was, to Hubbard, a no-brainer. Fletcher's life was in danger. The assailant had ignored repeated calls to scale back the confrontation, had shown no effects from the pepper spray. Hubbard pulled the trigger on his service revolver twice, fatally injuring Calloway.

Bang! Bang! Blake Hubbard's life had just changed forever, by forces over which he had zero control. Hubbard was on his way to a law-enforcement version of *The Twilight Zone*, where nothing seemed as it appeared.

Immediately, local prosecutors and the Grand Prairie police launched investigations into the shooting. Witnesses said that Hubbard had shouted obscenities at Calloway before shooting him; Hubbard, though few wanted to hear his version of what happened, said that was part of his police training.

"It's verbal judo, like the martial arts," he explained recently. "It's the way I was taught. If you talk like people talk on the streets, people will pay attention to you. You can say sit down a hundred times, and somebody might ignore you. You tell them 'sit the fuck down,' and people listen more."

A badly shaken Hubbard was barely able to drive his patrol car back to police headquarters, where he spoke with his superiors and came away convinced what he had done was the right thing. "They concluded an initial investigation, and word was the shooting appeared to be justified," he says now. That soon became official: A preliminary investigation by police determined it was a good shooting. The agreement of his superiors lifted somewhat the weight from Hubbard's shoulders.

"Personally, just me and the police chief, he was very supportive on that level," Hubbard remembers.

Blake Hubbard, in a one-minute exchange on a vacant lot, had just made the most difficult decision a police officer can ever face: to take the life of another human being in order to save the life of a fellow cop. He had the support of his bosses. Hubbard hoped to put the incident in the past, to continue working in the job that he loved so much.

It was not to be.

Race instantly became an issue in the Calloway shooting, with the Dallas chapter of the NAACP mounting demonstrations demanding a full investigation of the shooting and calling for an indictment. The head of the NAACP's local chapter, Lee Alcorn, became a constant, vocal presence, lobbying people in law enforcement to view Hubbard in a bad light. Sit-ins were staged at police headquarters and at a local television station, and protesters marched through the neighborhood proclaiming Hubbard's alleged police brutality.

Within a month of the shooting, those demonstrations were bearing fruit.

The FBI opened a civil rights investigation, raising the possibility of a federal case against Hubbard. And the police department was rethinking its initial conclusion. While a typical case like this would take less than a week, with the officer returned to duty, Hubbard spent a month on suspension while the probe continued. He started to get a queasy feeling.

Hubbard recalls walking through the Grand Prairie police station one day and encountering Police Chief Harry L. Crum, a man who had previously offered support.

"He put his head down and walked past me without saying anything," Hubbard says. "Prior to this, he was like, 'Hello, Blake, how are you?' I just felt this was weird. You know, that's kind of strange. You want him to see your face, know that you're still around. But he hustled by real fast. I thought that was strange. It left me with an uneasy feeling."

That feeling was justified. Within one month of the shooting, Hubbard was dealt a double dose of bad news from the very people he had once worked so closely with—the police and the prosecutors.

On November 6, 1996, the same police investigators who had initially told Hubbard that his actions were justified announced that Hubbard had been fired from the only job that he had ever wanted in life. Their probe found that Hubbard and Fletcher faced "no imminent danger" from the knife-wielding man. That finding was based in part on a statement from Fletcher—a statement that the officer would later disavow from the witness stand when he accused Chief Crum's right-hand man of twisting it against Hubbard.

"There is no question that Mr. Calloway had a knife in his hands, but an officer cannot use deadly force against another person unless there is an imminent threat," Crum said. "There was not an imminent threat when Officer Hubbard fired his weapon."

Who should define imminent threat—the officer in the field or the supervisor in the office? Experts have said a knife-wielding suspect standing as far as five feet away can be on top of a police officer in less than a quarter-second. Crum felt that was not imminent enough.

One day later, prosecutors announced Hubbard's indictment on murder charges by a grand jury that was not given the option of considering lesser charges such as manslaughter. No charges were brought against Fletcher.

"There's too much political pressure in this case for them to have done anything else," Read said later.

But prosecutors flatly denied that political pressure had anything to do with their decision to indict the twenty-seven-year-old police officer.

"This indictment is a result of facts presented to a grand jury," insisted Assistant District Attorney George West. "The grand jury made a fair determination of the issues."

NAACP head Alcorn didn't necessarily agree with that benign assessment.

"I can't say this is something that would have happened without some outside force," Alcorn said. "I think part of it was that they wanted to do the right thing, and part of it was we didn't give them the opportunity to cover up."

His statement begged the question: Cover up what? No one disputed that Calloway was waving a knife or behaving irrationally. There were witnesses, of course, who said that Calloway never made a move on Officer Fletcher, but the young cop—in a move that created quite a bit of controversy—defended Hubbard's response to this tense situation. There was, moreover, no weapon planted, no evidence of racial animus. Hubbard, rather than taking a confrontational stance in the wake of the slaying, made it clear that he was not sleeping well in the wake of his life-or-death decision.

"I wish this situation was different, so this would never have happened," Hubbard said.

But there was no denying it. It had happened, and it wasn't going to go away.

The negative comments also ignored Hubbard's pedigree, which was impressive to say the least. He was an Eagle Scout who was named to Who's Who Among American High School Students in both his junior and senior years at Harlingen High School. He worked his way through Stephen F. Austin University, graduating and joining the Grand Prairie PD in May 1994. He became a popular member of the police force, making friends and earning the respect of his fellow officers. He married his sweetheart Michelle, and they planned to start a family.

But Hubbard's present notoriety seemed to erase the past. He was the first person in twenty-four years to face charges in Dallas County of killing someone while on duty as a police officer. The decision to pursue Hubbard was not unprecedented, but it was surprising; in a previous case, a police officer questioning a suspect had placed a gun to the man's head and pulled the trigger. The cop said that he thought the gun was unloaded; he was convicted of murder, and wound up serving less than three years.

Hubbard, in contrast, faced a possible ninety-nine–year jail term for a shooting in considerably different circumstances. So different that it elicited this comment from him: "I was shocked that I was indicted at all."

In at least other three previous incidents, Texas police officers had been fired over controversial shootings but not indicted. Hubbard, it turned out, was getting the daily double—fired from his job, and faced with criminal charges.

"I was basically devastated," he said. "The career I had dreamed of was suddenly taken away. I was facing the possibility of going to prison for life. But I still believed I had done the right thing.

"It was a tragic thing. But it was the right thing."

Hubbard found solace in the support of his fellow law enforcers. The police brass had turned their backs on him, but a day never went by without one of his co-workers stopping by the house to offer encouragement or a pat on the back. Officers from around the country and around the world, angered that a cohort was being prosecuted for doing his job, called and wrote to let Hubbard know he wasn't alone; many of them helped out by contributing to his legal defense fund, a hedge against the soaring cost of defending himself.

Mark Clark, head of the Combined Law Enforcement Association of Texas (CLEAT), spoke for many when he ripped into the indictment.

"Never in my life have I heard of a police officer getting indicted for something like this," Clark fumed. "What kind of a message is this sending to a police officer out on the street? You have a situation where pepper spray and a baton were used and the person still has the deadly weapon. What in the hell is a police officer supposed to do? Wait to be cut?"

Ten days after the Texas jury indicted Blake Hubbard, two police officers in Ithaca, New York, responded to a call of an emotionally disturbed woman in her apartment building. Neighbors said she was talking to herself in a loud voice and creating a disturbance.

When police officer Michael Padula arrived, the woman was locked inside her bathroom. There was a standoff—until the woman threw open the bathroom door and plunged a knife into Padula's neck. The officer fell to the ground, dead. A second officer shot and killed the woman.

A grand jury voted no charges in this case.

Hubbard's first move in his efforts to vindicate his name and his actions was to hire Read, a Dallas attorney, who wasted no time in identifying his client's indictment as a political ploy based on racism.

"[Chief] Crum got on national television and said Hubbard used excessive force," Read said. "That's a bunch of bull and politics. He couldn't face the heat of all the protests, and the DA's office does what they have to do to appease politics. And now it has destroyed this guy's life.

"But now we're going to get it back."

Read also suggested that Hubbard had been targeted because of a previous incident: pulling over a black motorist on a routine traffic stop one year earlier. The driver was the president of a local bank, and he asserted that Hubbard and four other cops had harassed him. The man filed a $5 million suit against the city, the police department, and the five officers. It remains unresolved.

Within a week of his indictment, Hubbard surrendered on an arrest warrant in the very same building where he had once worked—Grand Prairie police headquarters. He was fingerprinted. Mug shots were taken. He spent one hour behind bars waiting for his attorney to post bail, sitting inside the same cell where he had once brought suspects.

"It was very humiliating," said the policeman turned prisoner. "One of the low spots."

Freed on bail, Hubbard steeled himself for his upcoming trial. In June 1997 he learned the stakes might be raised: Attorney Johnnie Cochran, Jr., best known for his criminal defense work for O. J. Simpson, was thinking about moving in and assisting the Calloway family. It seemed the evidence notwithstanding, the race card was about to be played, much to Hubbard's chagrin.

"I don't feel like this was an issue that race was involved in," Hubbard maintained. "It wasn't a factor. I felt that if the guy I shot was a white guy, or if I was a black cop, this wouldn't be happening."

But in the end, Hubbard didn't have to worry about Cochran. A federal judge blocked him from practicing law in Texas after finding that the lawyer's application failed to mention several grievances filed against him in other jurisdictions.

Read and Hubbard decided not to plead to a lesser charge than murder in return for a lesser sentence, or to fight to get the charges reduced; they would be satisfied only with an acquittal. It was a risky strategy, but they wanted the truth.

The trial—without Cochran—got under way on August 4, 1997, with the selection of a jury. It was a racially mixed panel of eleven women and one man: three blacks, one Hispanic, eight whites.

Read, outside the courthouse in Dallas, reiterated his beliefs: "This is politics." He defended his client as "a hardworking police officer who doesn't have a prejudiced bone in his body," and suggested the case had been brought only because his client was white.

The prosecutor charged Read with trying to "muddy up the waters. We're here to determine one thing—whether this is a murder or not."

Hubbard wanted the same thing. But the ex-cop had other things to think about, too. His wife had delivered their first child, a baby boy named Jacob, just one week before the start of his trial. Hubbard had to leave his infant son each morning and head for court to fight for his life.

The courtroom was packed with fellow cops and other supporters when the prosecution offered its case over two days. The prosecution witnesses called by Assistant District Attorney George West came up with not one single story that the cops used racial epithets or any indication that Calloway was killed because he was a black man. What they did testify to was that Calloway was not waving the knife at Fletcher, and that Calloway was standing a few feet away from the officers.

During the prosecution's case, the issue of race—which dominated most of the pretrial attention of the case—was not raised once.

The defense called Officer Barry Fletcher. His testimony helped turn the case around for Hubbard.

Fletcher said his sworn statements to police investigators, the documents that had been used to justify Hubbard's firing, were not "the whole truth." The statements that incriminated Hubbard, Fletcher said, had been made while internal affairs investigators were "hollering and screaming" at him. According to Fletcher, he was also given an incomplete state-ment to sign by Chief Crum's top assistant, and that statement was later amended to state that there was no reason for Hubbard to shoot at Calloway.

That, Fletcher said, was not true.

"If I had been in Officer Hubbard's situation and saw the knife move toward him, I would have shot [Calloway], too," said Fletcher. The officer also testified that he considered Hubbard a friend.

Hubbard walked to the witness stand on August 11, 1997, to tell the jury what had happened on that afternoon ten months before. Read, after watching the prosecution's case, said he believed that Hubbard didn't need to testify to win an acquittal.

"I don't think there's going to be enough evidence to convict my client," Read said bluntly, dismissing the case against Hubbard as "chicken manure." "But he needs to get up and tell everybody what happened for his own mental health," he added.

Hubbard detailed "an extremely volatile situation" involving his fellow officer and Calloway. He had testified in previous trials, but always as a law enforcer. Now he was a defendant. He remembers that the whole process was "nerve-wracking," because he was testifying to keep himself out of jail rather than put somebody else inside.

When Calloway made his third move at Fletcher, Hubbard told the jury, "I believed at that point there was no other option. My options were to allow him to attack Officer Fletcher or prevent it. It was my duty to protect Officer Fletcher's safety."

He finished testifying and returned to the defense table—what had for years been the other side of the courtroom, where the bad guys always sat. Read finished presenting his case, calling experts on the police force who testified that Hubbard's actions were good police procedure.

Both sides delivered their closing arguments.

On August 13, the jury started its deliberations. It took them only ninety minutes to clear Officer Blake Hubbard of the murder of Joseph Lee Calloway. The panel "did speak with one voice, and they feel good about their verdict," said state District Judge Janice Warder, who presided over the trial.

Hubbard stood outside the courtroom and declared, "I finally feel like I've been vindicated. I just did what I had to do."

Hubbard was cleared, but his fight was far from over. There was a threatened federal civil rights suit by Calloway's relatives that would likely name him. He wanted his job back, and that would entail another pitched legal fight.

"There's a lot of different reasons I want to get back on the job," Hubbard said recently. "My main reason is to clear my name, to show everybody I was right, to go back and pursue my career. A lot of my inspiration is from my kid, Jacob."

His trip through the legal system "has really had a devastating effect on my life and finances," Hubbard said. He's taken work as a private investigator while he awaits an arbitration hearing that will determine his future with the Grand Prairie police.

CLEAT head Clark believes that Hubbard should get that job back.

"He did precisely what he was trained to do," Clark said. "Grand Prairie's officers ought to be scratching their heads over what type of leadership they have."

Hubbard, who believes he was hung out to dry by the department's top officers, says there's one other reason that he's fighting: Nobody will do it for you.

"It's a reality I'm living with every day," he said. "And I will live with it every day of my life. But I was always confident that I would eventually win. I knew this was not murder, I knew I would be acquitted. And I'm still confident that I'll get my job back."

Hubbard, considering how draining the ordeal has been so far, sometimes has trouble convincing himself to keep on fighting.

"Some days are better than others," he said. "Some days my resolve wavers. But I am still ready to fight. I am still ready to do it."

*Chapter 8*

# THE SEARS CASE

## *HISTORY IN THE HEARTLAND*

**TODD SEARS, WHILE STILL** a probationary police officer, made Nebraska state history. It was a legacy he neither wanted nor expected when Sears entered law enforcement back in 1989.

Under a Nebraska law passed in 1988, a grand jury review of any police-involved death is required. Under that law, nine years after it passed, Todd Sears became the first officer ever indicted on felony criminal charges for an on-duty shooting incident, and only the third officer ever charged. An Omaha grand jury indicted Sears on manslaughter charges for shooting a man who pulled a gun on him one snowy October night as the officer and his partner responded to a report of an accident on the slippery roadways.

The man shot by Sears had more than twice the legal limit of alcohol in his system, and drug tests showed the presence of cocaine, too. The gun that the man was carrying was registered in his name; there was no doubt that it was his weapon, no allegations of a wrongful shooting and a planted gun—a fairly cut-and-dried case.

An internal police review cleared Sears. But apparently that wasn't enough in this case, which quickly became a cause célèbre.

Why? Why was the police shooting of an inebriated, gun-toting man characterized as a racial shooting?

Sears is white. The victim was black. And local minority leaders charged there was a pattern of police brutality against African-Americans by the Omaha Police Department. Sears became a scapegoat for the alleged past sins of police officers.

His supporters said there was one problem with that stance: it ignored the facts in the case. And because of that, Todd Sears now faces up to twenty years behind bars.

"His actions don't come within a mile of a criminal charge," said his disbelieving attorney, John Fahey, who works for the local police union.

It was shortly after 1:30 AM on October 26, 1997, when a call came out from the Omaha police dispatch. There was an accident at 65th Street and Hartman Avenue on a night ripe for fender-benders—a snowstorm that would knock out power to 100,000 people was blowing in. Two units responded to the accident call. On of the cars contained Officer Troy Kister, who was riding with an officer-in-training—Todd Sears.

Sears, thirty-three, was born in southern Omaha. He joined the Sarpy County sheriff's department in 1989, and spent the next seven years there. He opted to make the leap from sheriff's department to the Omaha PD in 1997, looking for higher pay and better benefits. When he graduated second in his class from the police academy in February 1997, his brother Preston was already an eleven-year veteran of the Omaha force.

When he was a deputy sheriff, Sears had made headlines with the daring rescue of a woman from a burning apartment building in 1995. Despite smoke and flames that drove other would-be rescuers back, Sears charged up the stairs to a second-floor apartment and carried sixty-five-year-old Jean Kelly from her burning home to safety. Sears, who suffered burns on his hands and smoke inhalation, received the department's Life Saving Award.

He was a fan of Nebraska Cornhusker football, and watched the games with a group of friends at a local bar. One of his friends, a black man named Jeff Noble, said he had never heard Sears utter a racial epithet.

> **The officer then fired a blast of pepper spray at the suspect, but he appeared immune to the noxious mixture and went on waving the knife and rambling.**

Co-workers uniformly praised Sears' police work. "As good a police officer as I've ever worked with," said Steve Grabowski, a lieutenant with the sheriff's department.

"Dedicated to helping people out," agreed police detective David Bruck.

Sears has a girlfriend; they have been together for eight years, and friends say he is like a father to her ten-year-old son. Also, as an ex-wrestler, Sears helped coach wrestling and baseball in a town outside of Omaha.

After graduating from the Omaha police academy, Sears failed a physical and nearly lost his job. He challenged the results of the physical and was reinstated in August, two months before the routine traffic call that would turn his life topsy-turvy.

His partner, Kister, had matched Sears in the life-saving department. In January 1997, Kourtney and Jennifer Woracek—three-year-old twins—had wandered out of their home and into subzero temperatures. Kister had spotted their tiny footprints in the snow and tracked the missing girls down.

The dispatcher reported that the accident on Hartman Avenue involved a white 1997 Grand Am and a late-model red Chevrolet Camaro. One of the drivers had called police on his cellular phone to report the accident. The call came at 1:20 AM; four minutes later, Sears and Kister were on their way to the scene.

At 1:29 AM the officers spotted two other cars— Ammons's sport utility vehicle was one of them—stopped on the side of the road two blocks from the reported accident scene. Unsure if this was another accident, Kister flipped on the police car's lights and pulled over. One of the two cars drove off as the officers arrived at the scene. The officers saw no damage on the car left behind, and determined it was not an accident. At this point, they had no idea what they were dealing with here.

"There were just stopping to ask, 'Hey, did you get in a car wreck?'" police spokesman Sgt. Jim Deignan would say later.

Sears, with his case still pending, declined through his attorney to discuss what happened that night. But his girl-friend, Cathleen Peters, told this version of the story to his supporters in a letter aimed at raising funds for Sears's legal defense: "Nothing could have prepared him and his partner for what was about to happen," she wrote. "It was 1:30 in the morning, and the snow was blinding."

The driver of the remaining car, Marvin Ammons, left his vehicle and walked around to the police car's passenger side. Ammons had just turned thirty-three, and he had spent most of Saturday evening celebrating with cocktails at Cleopatra's Lounge.

Ammons, who grew up in northern Omaha, was a Gulf War veteran now working as a city bus driver. His blood alcohol level was .203, more than double the legal limit for dri-ving. An autopsy would turn up traces of cocaine in his system.

Kister, sitting in the driver's seat of the patrol car, leaned across his partner and asked Ammons if there had been an accident. Ammons, now standing alongside the police cruiser, said no. And then the officers both noticed the weapon that Marvin Ammons had holstered in the waistband of his pants.

"Officer Kister shouted, 'GUN!', and Todd [Sears] ordered the main to raise his arms," Peters wrote. "Todd drew his gun and pleaded with the man not to draw his. Todd screamed at him over and over, 'Don't do it! Don't do it!'"

"But the suspect drew his gun anyway and began swing-ing it toward Todd's head." Sears, in the passenger's seat, pulled his gun and fired three shots. Two of them struck

Ammons in the chest. It was the first time that he had fired his weapon on the job in a decade of police work.

"We got shots fired, persons down at 63rd and Hartman," came the radio call from Kister's unit, 1 Adam 33. "I got a person down in an officer-related shooting."

Ammons's gun was found on the ground near his right hand. Marvin Ammons was pronounced dead at St. Joseph Hospital about thirty minutes later.

Lieutenant David Friend, the head of the local police union, said there was no doubt that the shooting was justified. "Sears had no avenue of escape.... The only choice Sears had was to use lethal force," Friend said.

The union official compared Sears's situation to the 1995 case of Omaha Police Officer Jimmy Wilson, Jr., who was killed during a routine traffic stop. Wilson was sitting in his cruiser's front seat when the driver of the stopped car pulled a weapon and shot him to death.

Sears "tells me all he can think of is Jimmy Wilson, where he doesn't even get a chance to get out of his car," Friend said. He adds that Sears wasn't alone in feeling intimidated by Ammons's actions that morning—Kister had pulled his handgun as well. "Sears had no choice in the matter," the lieutenant said.

Even if Ammons had simply intended to turn his gun over to the officers, the two cops had no way of reading his mind, of determining his intent, Friend said.

"The best-case scenario shows a lack of judgment [by Ammons]," Friend said. "The worst case shows intent of malice toward the officer. We will never know what his intentions were. It's a tragedy. But the officer didn't do anything wrong."

That wasn't Friend's call to make. Instead, there was a police investigation, a grand jury investigation, and an FBI investigation.

It took only three days for the hindsight patrol to begin questioning Sears's decision. He was soon second-guessed more than a football coach with a ten-game losing streak.

A city councilman raised the first question. Why had Sears's partner turned off the video camera installed on his patrol car? The camera could have provided undeniable evidence of what had happened between Ammons and the officers. Kistler, believing this was nothing more than a routine traffic accident, had turned the camera off once they arrived at the scene.

Oklahoma State Sen. Ernie Chambers issued an appeal for the U.S. attorney's office to investigate the case, suggesting just five days after the shooting—before there was even an official police finding on the case—that there was "a cover-up of wrongful conduct."

Chambers, in addition to his call for federal intervention, launched an assault on Omaha mayor Hal Daub. He accused the mayor of lobbying the city's residents "to accept official exoneration of a wrong-doing cop." A Daub spokesman shot back that Chambers was running his mouth without waiting for the completion of the investigation.

Either way, this was no longer a simple probe of a police shooting; it was now, befitting the heartland home of legendary Nebraska coach Tom Osborne, a political football.

The police union came forward with a November 3 news conference to defend Sears. But two days later, the U.S.

Attorney—responding to Chambers's call—announced that the FBI would mount a probe. A statement from George Andrew, special agent in charge of the FBI's Omaha office, acknowledged "the various state and local investigations which are under way," but said "public confidence would be best served" by another look at the case.

"It became a war of words," said the Rev. Larry Menyweather-Woods, pastor of Ammons's church. "For many of us in the black community, it was a matter of high suspicion. There's been a history, a bad relationship with the police an the community across the years."

Exacerbating tensions was a bitter, public fight between Ammons's mother and the city over access to evidence surrounding the shooting. The city maintained that Ollie Reaves, the slain man's mother, wasn't entitled to see the evidence because she had not filed a lawsuit in the case and because it could taint the upcoming grand jury probe. Emotions ran high, as Ms. Reaves insisted, "I want to know how he died, and that's all." This protracted battle went all the way to the Nebraska Supreme Court before it was resolved in favor of Ammons's family.

Sears, the focus of all this unrest, was placed in a desk job. He became a fixture at Central Police Headquarters, taken off the streets until there was a resolution of his case. A month after the high school protest, local activists turned up the heat with another session at an Omaha church. Religious leaders held a news conference demanding that the city surrender all the evidence to Ms. Reaves. Ammons's brother, charging Omaha officials were prejudiced in favor of the police, demanded a special prosecutor's ouster in favor of an independent prosecutor.

In a bizarre ruling that seemed to contradict itself, Douglas County District Court Judge Joseph Troia heeded their calls and appointed a special prosecutor. While Troia expressed "the highest confidence" that local prosecutors could handle the case, the judge decided it was "in the best interest of the community" that an outside lawyer handle the case.

The decision had "no substance, no legal reasoning," said an editorial in the Omaha World-Herald. "...A judge who exercises 'inherent judicial power' ought to explain himself."

It was only the second time since the Nebraska law, introduced by Sen. Chambers, had resulted in the appointment of a special prosecutor. In 1994 a man named Francisco Renteria died after a struggle with two officers in Lincoln, Nebraska. The cops were indicted on misdemeanor charges and acquitted.

Initially, it seemed that Sears's case might not go that far. In January, the first probe that was launched—an internal police investigation—reached its conclusion: Sears had acted within police guidelines when he pulled the trigger. The report, made public January 6, declared that Sears had followed police procedures and did not use excessive force during his showdown with Marvin Ammons.

It was the first good news for Sears in several months. But one day earlier, after a short delay so its members could watch Nebraska in the Orange Bowl, the grand jury had started its work. They soon delivered Sears the worst news that he could have received.

On January 26, 1998, the grand jury announced that it had indicted Sears. Over three weeks, they had heard from 50 witnesses and reviewed 228 exhibits. It later turned out that 2 of the jurors had ignored the judge's orders and turned amateur Colombos, visiting the crime scene to conduct their own investigation—a clear case of juror misconduct.

Only twelve of the sixteen jurors had to agree on the indictment; their first vote came up short of that number, one of the panel later said, but they voted a second time after some additional discussion. The special prosecutor, John P. Grant, refused to say if their decision was unanimous, but the jury ultimately decided that Sears had caused "the death of Marvin D. Ammons without malice... while in the commission of an unlawful act."

Sears's family, friends, and legal team were stunned by the decision. Sears, while on duty, had simply stopped to check out a possible accident—that was undisputed. Ammons was carrying a gun. Sears's attorney, Fahey, was livid, asserting emphatically that his client had done no wrong.

"I'm disgusted," Fahey fumed. "This is disgusting." Fahey said his client had become a political scapegoat, an unwitting victim of the system and local politics.

"This thing got its start because of all the secrecy and the cloud of suspicion that hung over these two guys who didn't do anything but their job and put themselves in harm's way," Fahey continued. "It's been built up by hysteria, misrepresentation. We've indicted an innocent man."

It was Fahey who had to deliver the grand jury's decision to Sears. The officer's reaction? "He is astounded—as we are, as anybody connected with police work would be," the lawyer said.

The grand jury, rather than focusing on Sears's actions, said it was troubled by a variety of actions that accompanied the actual shooting: Kister's decision to turn off the video camera; how Ammons's cellular phone wound up in the officers' patrol car; why the officers on the scene communicated via their cellular phones rather than police radio.

One juror, speaking on condition of anonymity, told the Omaha World-Herald that a police report asserting that Sears had used the word "nigger" during a police training class worked against the officer. The juror said the shooting case had "too many loose ends," although she later said those could be the result of sloppy police work.

That was enough to indict, the juror said.

Others seemed confused by the jury's logic. A spokesman for Mayor Daub characterized the indictment as "puzzling and surprising, to say the least."

Sears had a new reason to arrive at Central Police Headquarters: the officer had to surrender for booking on the manslaughter charges. The tables were turned—he posed for mug shots, provided fingerprints. But he didn't lose the support of his fellow cops.

"I'm behind Officer Sears 100 percent," said Omaha's acting police chief, Charlie Circo. "I believe he's going to be found not guilty."

Circo placed the blame for the shooting squarely on Ammons, rather than on Sears: "Had there not been a gun in Mr. Ammons's belt, we would not be here today."

When Sears had his first court appearance in late January, the courtroom was a sea of blue: more than 150 uniform-clad officers in a public show of support for their comrade, filling the pews and standing against the courtroom walls. Douglas County District Judge Robert Burkhard released him without any bail; at his next hearing, Sears entered a plea of not guilty. The officer maintained his public silence on the case, not even uttering a word in court. But friends and supporters said he was anxious to clear his name.

"Officer Sears," said attorney Greg Abboud, "is looking forward to his day in court."

Sears's new lawyer, Mike Fabian, has asked that the officer's indictment be dismissed because of the jurors' misconduct. Depending on the ruling, Sears could walk free, or face a trial at some point, or become the focus of a second grand jury.

As often happens in these volatile cases, Ammons's family filed paperwork for a civil suit in the case. Interestingly, though, they did not sue Sears or the police department for wrongful death. Instead, their $750,000 suit claimed that the family was caused undue emotional distress when city and court officials refused to tell them the exact circumstances of Ammons's death, and that officials kept them from viewing the dead man's body for two days after the shooting.

Sears's criminal trial could force a delay of his scheduled 1999 marriage to Cathleen Peters. It should also answer the grand jury's questions about the shooting, although at least one police investigator feels that the panel focused on the wrong questions.

Captain Anthony Infantino, who handled the police problem of the shooting, said the important questions in the case
will never have answers:

"Why was Mr. Ammons carrying a gun? Why did Mr.
Ammons reach for the gun? Those are questions that can
never be answered."

*Chapter 7*

# THE KING CASE

## *THE MOTHER OF THEM ALL*

**HE DIDN'T CARRY A GUN.** He didn't wear a badge. He never went through the police academy.

But Rodney King changed the way police did business across this country. His brutal arrest after a high-speed chase through Los Angeles, captured on a videotape played endlessly on television (and later included in a Spike Lee film), made the Rodney King case the mother of all police brutality cases in the 1990s. It changed the way that the police operated, the way prosecutors operated, and the way politicians viewed such volatile cases.

Nothing was the same in the law enforcement business after the smoke above Los Angeles cleared following the worst urban rioting since the late 1960s.

The details of the King case are familiar to most—at least the details as they were initially presented, since a pair of trials (one state, one federal) presented two different juries with different scenarios as to what really happened that night out-side the Hansen Dam Recreational Park.

Rodney King was driving erratically at speeds of up to 100 mph when the California Highway Patrol attempted to pull his car over. King instead led them on a wild eight-mile chase, finally stopping just outside the entrance to a local park.

Two passengers in King's car obeyed the order of police to exit the car and lie face down on the ground. Both were handcuffed and taken into custody without incident.

King did not acquiesce, despite repeated commands to get down on the ground and place his hands in the small of his back. LAPD police officers Lawrence Powell, Timothy Wind, and Theodore Briseno moved in to arrest King, but the suspect was able to fight them off. Sgt. Stacey Koon twice attempted to bring the suspect down with taser shots, hitting King with 50,000 volts of electricity. Koon later recalled that they seemed to have no effect on King, who showed no signs of obeying the orders or giving up the fight.

The police believed the 6-foot-2, 240-pound King was probably high on PCP, based on his bizarre behavior and his extraordinary strength. "He's turned into the Hulk," Koon later recalled thinking.

At this point, two things happened: Koon ordered his officers to use their police-issue PR 24 metal batons on Rodney King. And George Holliday, who had noticed the ruckus outside his apartment, decided to flip on his new videocamera and record the arrest.

The eighty-two–second videotape showed the white offi-cers landing blow after blow on the seemingly helpless black man—King's attorney would later estimate fifty-six, Koon later put the number at thirty-three. Koon said that once every six seconds, he ordered King to surrender.

Never did the suspect obey.

King was finally arrested after holding his hands in the air and telling the cops, "Please stop." Even at this point, when surrendering, King refused to follow orders to lie face down.

"We were astonished," Koon later wrote in his book, *Presumed Guilty.* "We had never seen anything like it before. We had never encountered a suspect who could absorb the number of power strokes Rodney King had taken to his legs, arms, and torso and not show any pain.

"This was a nightmarish reality, completely contrary to our training."

On his way to the hospital, King kept spitting at a police officer riding in the ambulance, repeatedly telling her, "Fuck you." During his arrest, King suffered bruises on his face, lacerations to his right cheekbone and chin, a fractured cheekbone, and a small fracture of his right fibula.

Taken at face value, the videotape seemed incontrovertible: This was something out of a deep South sheriff's office back in the early 1960s, racist cops getting their jollies by beating the hell out of some black man who was just in the wrong place at the wrong time. King added fuel to the racial fire by telling investigators that the officers had directed racial slurs at him while they were hitting him with their batons. (King's claim was never substantiated, and an enhanced review of the Holliday tape's audio turned up nothing more than Koon's oft-repeated orders to surrender. Though the racial aspect of the beating was frequently played up in stories about the case and by King's supporters, no evidence was ever produced that the arrest/attack was racially motivated.)

The officers saw the videotape a different way. They would later argue—successfully, in a criminal trial—that the videotape alone was totally out of context. It needed to be seen in connection with what had happened before—the chase, the violent fight, the repeated refusal to cooperate with the officers.

Few seemed to agree with the cops' position.

A Los Angeles Times columnist described the cops as "Ku Klux Klanners on a feeding frenzy… (taking) turns kicking and whacking him with nightsticks." Mayor Tom Bradley—in a move that foreshadowed the response of other politicians put in the same position through the '90s—wasted no time in convicting the officers without waiting for trial. Bradley didn't consider the possibility that the officers might be innocent; their conviction was simply "a matter of identifying and finding witnesses," he said.

All four officers were indicted on criminal charges. Koon, Powell, and Briseno were suspended without pay on March 15, 1991. That same day, Wind—who was still a probationary officer—was fired.

The cops were now the crooks. And the suspect, Rodney King, was now something of a cult hero and a symbol of racial injustice.

As it turned out, Bradley was wrong. The cops asked for a change of venue, arguing that comments like Bradley's would make a fair trial in Los Angeles impossible. A judge agreed, and the case was moved to suburban Simi Valley, California.

The jury there heard from Sergeant Koon, who did a frame-by-frame review of the Holliday videotape to bolster his claim that the officers had no choice but to use extreme force as a final option on King. Under cross-examination, the prosecutor asked Koon, "Did Mr. King have any weapons?"

"Yes," Koon shot back. "His body, under the influence of PCP."

No tests ever confirmed Koon's belief about King's drug use. But the sergeant certainly gave the jurors a portrait of Rodney King far different from that shown in the eighty-two–second videotape.

After a four-week trial, the jury spent seven days deliberating. At 3:15 PM on April 29, 1992, the jury acquitted Koon, Briseno, and Wind. There was a hung jury for Powell, with the panel split 8-4 in favor of acquittal.

For those who were not at the trial every day, for those whose knowledge of the case was provided solely by the Holliday tape, the verdict seemed a miscarriage of justice. President Bush summed it up this way: "Viewed from outside the trial, it was hard to understand how the verdict could possibly square with the videotape."

Which is precisely the point—the ultimate decision rested not with the trial's outsiders, but with the jury, which heard all the evidence, viewed the full videotape, listened to the testimony, and acquitted the officers.

The rioting started hours after the jury returned, another event that would color the handling of such cases through the

'90s—politicians quick to turn against accused cops, desperate to prevent their cities from going up in flames.

The Foothill Four, as the King cops were dubbed—they worked out of the Foothill Division headquarters—wound up facing two more trials. There was a federal case alleging that King's civil rights were violated on the night of his arrest; supporters of the cops called it double jeopardy, while King's supporters labeled it justice. The federal case ended with convictions for Powell and Koon; each was sentenced to thirty months behind bars.

The civil case—which received very little attention compared to the other two trials—had an interesting verdict. The same jury that heard the case against the officers had ordered the city of Los Angeles to pay Rodney King a total of $3.8 million. Yet they decided that the officers involved in the case did not owe King one cent in damages.

"There was no doubt in my mind that Mr. King was at fault for a good deal of what happened," one juror told the Los Angeles Times. "The police officers were using the tools they had been given."

The King case was like a Pandora's box of brutality—once it was opened, nothing would ever be the same. Echoes of the King case reverberate throughout the cases of Nevers and Budzyn in Detroit; Mulholland and company in Pittsburgh; Hubbard in Grand Prairie, Texas; Leaks in Newark, New Jersey.

The politics of race? The King case had it.

The near-instant conviction of a cop without even the presumption of innocence? The King case had it.

Back-pedaling politicians and police brass. Dramatic trials. Massive media coverage. Other cop cases had them, but the King case had it first.

# EPILOGUE

**SEVEN YEARS AFTER RODNEY KING,** six years after Nevers and Budzyn, three years after Jonny Gammage, the debate rages on—the second guessing continues, the speculation endures about what constitutes police brutality. Cops and their constituents are often at odds over the way police do their jobs, or—in some cases—the perception of how police do their jobs. The police rank and file, in many instances, feel that they are held to a different standard, and that politics more often than not influence the handling of any case involving a uniform.

"That's what you get for being a cop, right?" Joe Mancini, spokesman for the 29,000-member New York Patrolmen's Benevolent Assocation (PBA), observed drily one May afternoon. Hours earlier, a Brooklyn cop—a PBA delegate—had died of gunshot wounds in a city hospital.

Police union officials in cities troubled by high-profile police trials that divided the community say the cases often leave lasting scars among officers who lay their lives on the line every day for the very same people who protest against them.

The feeling that they were hung out to dry, or offered up as scapegoats simply for doing their jobs, spreads quickly through the often-insular departments. The officers' discussions, union officials say, often ends with one question: "Who's next?"

Speaking about the repercussions of the King case, Los Angeles Police Protective League President Dave Hepburn said he could discern a long-term effect on his union's members.

"There's an impact on morale," said Hepburn, whose group offered financial aid to the four officers charged in the King case. "There's an impact on how aggressive the police are, how far they will put themselves out on a limb to do the job.

"If you get together any group of policemen, that's always one of the topics of discussion. I don't like to say it, but they wonder: 'Why stick out your neck? If you don't get involved, the pay is the same. Why take the chance of getting prosecuted, sued, losing your job?'

"There are so many negative consequences for sticking out your neck, and none for not."

Increasingly, there are calls for outside, independent investigations of police misconduct—an area that was once exclusively the domain of the police departments themselves. In New York City, a Civilian Complaint Review Board was created to handle citizens' complaints of police wrongdoing.

Not everyone agreed with its creation.

New York City Mayor Rudolph Giuliani has presided over one of the most stunning reversals in U.S. law enforcement history, turning the Big Apple into one of the nation's safest major cities. It was a turnaround that appeared improbable, if not impossible, at the start of the decade.

During Giuliani's first four-year term, crime statistics showed a staggering decrease. The murder count in 1997 was 767, the lowest since 1967. In 1990 there were nearly three times as many homicides: 2,245.

Auto theft, burglary, robbery, rape, assault, grand larceny—all these areas of crime showed a sharp downturn between 1993 and 1997. Under the Giuliani administration, crime tumbled by more than 40 percent across the board, the statistics showed.

In 1997, as he headed toward re-election, Giuliani took a major political hit when a Haitian immigrant was allegedly assaulted inside a Brooklyn police precinct by four officers. The victim was sodomized with a wooden stick and beaten within an inch of his life. Critics of the mayor said his attitude toward the police, giving them unwavering support, had created an atmosphere where the officers felt they were above the law in dealing with criminal suspects.

Giuliani angrily disagreed. But despite the criticism, he remained unwavering in one position: The best way of policing any police department is keeping everything in house.

"I continue to believe," Giuliani said in September 1997, "that the most effective way to investigate police misconduct is to do it within the Police Department."

Guilt or innocence is a question that can be answered by a jury. An officers' reputation? That's harder to determine or protect.

In November 1997 two New York City police officers were identified in a newspaper article in which a Hispanic couple claimed they were attacked for arguing a parking ticket. A Manhattan dentist and his girlfriend accused the two officers of smashing them with police radios, then dragging them into the local precinct house. There, the pair said, the officers stripped them and beat them once again.

In the wake of the Brooklyn attack, the story raised further questions about police brutality and relationships between the police and the Latino community. The Manhattan district attorney investigated, as did the police Internal Affairs Bureau.

A grand jury was convened, and it returned an indictment—against the dentist and the girlfriend, who were accused of resisting arrest and falsely reporting an incident. According to the indictment, the dentist and his girlfriend attacked the two officers. Both cops were exonerated by the investigation—months after the original report.

"Punish the Cop Slanderers!" the *New York Post* thundered in an editorial. "Charges of police brutality are depressingly common," the editorial continued. "Sometimes... the charges seem to have substance. More often, however, such allegations seem embellished, or even fabricated, as some kind of a twisted revenge for past grievances—or in hopes of hitting the litigation lottery."

The suspects could have sued the cops. Where do the cops turn once the story is exposed as being phony?

In the end, all the talk about cops' behavior is mostly rhetoric, according to Hepburn. Second-guessing or not, any internal struggles aside, the vast majority of cops are police officers first. Everything else runs a distant second.

Once they put on the uniform, a cop's instincts take over.

"Cops being cops, they enjoy doing their job," Hepburn said. "And most will continue to do those jobs, no matter what happens."

# INDEX

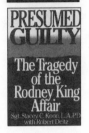

# Also by Regnery Publishing...

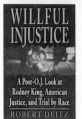
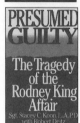